D1573024

ATTACK HELICOPTERS

ATTACK HELICOPTERS

A History of Rotary-Wing Combat Aircraft

HOWARD A. WHEELER

The Nautical and Aviation Publishing Company of America
Baltimore, Maryland

 All inquiries should be sent to The Nautical & Aviation Publishing Company of America, 101 West Read Street, Suite 314, Baltimore, Maryland 21201.

ISBN: 0-933852-52-5

Library of Congress Catalog No.: 87-24900

Printed in the United States of America
First printing 1987

Library of Congress Cataloging-in-Publication Data
Wheeler, Howard A.
Attack helicopters.
Bibliography: p.
Includes index.
1. Attack helicopters—History, I. Title.
UG1230.G47 1987 358.4′183 87-24900
ISBN 0-933852-52-5

All pictures are United States Department of Defense photographs unless otherwise identified.

Dedication

To JoEllen

CONTENTS

ACKNOWLEDGEMENTS

I would like to express my sincere thanks to the following people who offered me enthusiastic encouragement, thoughtful advice and technical information: Captain Richard C. Knott, USN (Ret.); Commander Peter B. Mersky, USNR-R; Mrs. Helen Collins; Mr. Terry C. Tradwell; Lieutenant Commander Allan S. Conrad, USN; Lieutenant Colonel Frank M. Brewer, USMC; Commander Paul Madge, Royal Navy, Fleet Air Arm Public Affairs; Lieutenant Commander and Mrs. "Will" Hollowell, USN; Mr. A. "Mike" Leahy; Senior Chief Journalist Kirby Harrison, USN (Ret.); Mr. Timothy J. Christmann; Mr. Roy Grossnick, Naval Aviation Historian; Mr. John M. Elliott, Assistant Naval Aviation Historian; Mr. Robert F. Dorr; Mrs. Gwendolyn Rich, Naval Aviation History Archives; Mrs. Sandy Russell, Managing Editor, *Naval Aviation News*; Mr. Vincent H. Demma, U.S. Army Center for Military History; Captain Rosario "Zip" Rausa, USNR; Mr. Graham Mottram, Curator, and Commander Dennis White, RN (Ret.), Director, Fleet Air Arm Museum, Royal Naval Air Station, Yeovilton; Mr. Phillip Edwards, National Air & Space Museum Reference Library; Mr. David Dorrell, Editor, *Air Pictorial Magazine*; Mr. David Brown, Historian, Royal Naval Historical Branch; Mr. Richard T. Riding, Editor, *Aeroplane Monthly*; Mr. Barry Wheeler, Editor, Joint Services Recognition Journal; Mr. Alan Hall, Publisher, *Aviation News*; Mr. Gordon Swanborough, Pilot Press; Mr. Paul Beaver, Editor, *Defence Helicopter World*; Mr. Mike Gibb, Hughes Helicopter Inc.; Ms. Madelyn Bush, Boeing Vertol Company; Kaman Aerospace, Inc.; Commander Nigel "Sharky" Ward, Royal Navy; Mr. Robert F. Dorr; Captain Arne Bruflat, USN; Captain James L. Hughes, USN; and Mr. Norman Polmar.

INTRODUCTION

The fragile helicopters, their rotor blades gently drooping to the gusts of cold November wind, were dwarfed by the giant airship hangars at the Naval Air Station in Lakehurst, New Jersey. The helicopters' crew members were thoroughly chilled by the winter wind on that frigid day in 1950. It was not a routine day on the flight line, but no day is ever routine for helicopter crews. And for the masters of these relatively new, and to some, strange, flying machines it was to be a busy day of test and evaluation.

These machines were special. They were Sikorsky HO3S-1s, one of the best helicopters the Navy had. The squadron they belonged to was the Navy's first of its kind, Helicopter Utility Squadron One (HU-1), commissioned on that base on April 1, 1948.

The mechanics and pilots of HU-1 struggled with one of the lightweight HO3S-1s. What these industrious men were doing was unofficial; it was a day of experimentation.

Somebody had figured that if helicopters could haul litter, patients, cargo and the mail, surely they could play a more active role in time of war, perhaps as airborne fighting machines. They thought the HO3S-1 would be a good test bed for their experiment even though its R-985-AN-5 Wasp Junior 450-hp radial engine always strained to lift the 4985 pound airframe off the ground. It had little power left to get the pilot and his crew out of tight situations. It took a good deal of skill to fly these relatively unstable birds.

Nevertheless, the crew removed the doors and juryrigged swivel gun mounts in their place on each side of the narrow fuselage. On the gun mounts they attached .30- and .50-caliber machine guns.

The setup looked good, but the experiment proved that it was an idea that had come before its time. The recoil of the heavy automatic machine guns nearly tore the sides off the fuselage. Their ingenuity was years ahead of helicopter design technology. Thus ended one of the first experiments in firing machine guns from helicopters.

The history of attack helicopters is as much about the pilots, flight-crew, inventors and engineers as it is about the incredible vertical flying machines themselves. The story begins with man's dream to fly like the birds, enjoying their freedom of going aloft at will and landing virtually anywhere, and unfolds with the genius of many minds dedicated to solving the technical problems of vertical flight. After centuries of curiosity, study, experimentation and failures, the goal was finally achieved with the invention of a very unique aircraft—the helicopter.

Indeed, with the helicopter we have the freedom to take off when we want, fly great distances and, with a few limitations, land anywhere we wish—even on water. With this remarkable vehicle at our disposal, we now enjoy unsurpassed mobility.

Those who have piloted a helicopter, mastered its many unique flight characteristics and have flown it against an enemy in combat fully understand its immense capabilities and usefulness. There is no feeling like being at the controls of a helicopter flying close to the earth or hovering. It instills an overwhelming sense of power. Only the relatively small fraternity of rotary-wing aviators can fully appreciate the many virtues of modern helicopters.

Helicopters are one of the most versatile and yet, in an aerodynamic sense, the least understood of our flying machines. In recent years, rotary-wing aircraft have gained the lion's share of the glamour and recognition that fixed-wing aircraft have enjoyed since the Wright brothers made aviation history at Kitty Hawk. This is particularly true for armed helicopters; it took more than two decades for them to be fully integrated into the battlefield scenario both on land and at sea.

During the late 1940s through the 1950s, the helicopter's capabilities were greatly underestimated by military tacticians and planners: their potential was not aggressively explored, and they were not designed and built properly to face the rigors of battle. They were manufactured and placed in combat with many limitations in speed, load capacity, range and endurance. These limitations contributed to their lack of acceptance by local commanders, and so they did not receive proper recognition for what they were able to do. Relegated to general duties such as logistics and search and rescue, it would take decades for them to evolve into high-technology aircraft.

With today's methodical procurement procedures and highly advanced technologies, rotary-wing aircraft are vital to military forces. The ability to land and take off without dependence on runways or the arresting gear and catapults of aircraft carriers makes them well adapted and necessary to modern warfare.

War has inspired many of our most impressive inventions. Unlike most military inventions, which were designed either for projecting firepower or defending against the enemy, the helicopter began its military career as a life saver: it was used for medical evacuation (medevac).

In the developmental years, the growth of rotary-wing technology must be attributed to scientists from many nations, most notably Germany, France, England, the United States and the Soviet Union. Had the helicopter depended upon commercial use for its development, we would probably still be flying autogiros today. Fortunately, there were leaders within the military organizations of these nations with the imagination and vision to support the exploration of rotary-wing technology.

Military aviators are special people, endowed by their Creator with unique mental and physical attributes that set them a cut above ordinary mortals, and they know it! They all have that something extra that enables them to absorb the most intensive and demanding course of instruction conceived by man. Some are better than others, some more daring than others, but they all have the skill and determination to get the job done, no matter what that job might be![1]

Thus stated Chief Warrant Officer Fourth Class Michael J. Novosel, the oldest active duty member of the U.S. Army to receive the Medal of Honor for his Vietnam service. He was on duty when the Japanese bombed Pearl Harbor and served in Vietnam as a "Dustoff" mission of mercy helicopter pilot during which he extracted more than fifty-five hundred soldiers and civilians. He witnessed much of the Army's helicopter aviation history.

While the soldier is the most important element in warfare, it takes much more than troops to win. Having the right equipment, transportation and training come together at the proper time to operate in whatever conditions are at hand makes the difference between winning and losing. This is where the helicopter plays a major role.

One theorist postulated that the individual who controls the sky, controls the world. While this is debatable in terms of global warfare, it is certainly true when applied to the battlefield. Air superiority is a must in any firefight because the side that controls the air over the combat zone has the greatest offensive advantage.

But there is more to war than controlling the air space above the combat area. Mobility of forces is also an important factor.

> Transportation throughout the ages has significantly affected the outcome of famous military campaigns. Victory has usually gone to the armies which have been able to move most swiftly.[2]

Alexander's phalanx, Hannibal's elephants and Genghis Khan's cavalry were all contributors to the strength of their respective armies. Mobility has always been one of the strongest elements of victory, and in modern warfare the helicopter has proven to be capable of fulfilling this need most admirably.

While transporting troops to the scene of the action is an important mission, transporting the wounded out is of equal importance. Medical evacuation and search and rescue (SAR) will always be among the helicopter's most important duties. The early medevac experiments late in World War II, during the Malayan Emergency (in the early 1950s) and during the Korean War were early testimony to this capability of helicopters. Additionally, on numerous occasions the civilian populace has benefited from its lifesaving capabilities during natural disasters.

The combat helicopter adds much to the basic military principles of independence of action, concentration of effort, efficiency of forces, security, mobility and rapid intervention by the troops on the ground.[3] When all of these factors are satisfied, the chance of victory in battle is greatly enhanced.

Improvements in technology gave inventors and engineers the opportunities needed to refine their early designs and make this aircraft a reliable and effective fighting machine. As early as the 1920s, the concept of vertical rotary-wing flight had been proven; that is, models could be designed and flown, but that was about all. Little progress could be realized until sufficient power became available. Most of the power and flight control problems were not solved until the early 1950s, which is when helicopters began to be widely used both in civilian and military applications.

Perhaps the single most important catalyst that contributed to the long awaited development of the practical helicopter was the internal combustion engine. First there was the gasoline piston engine, followed by the gas turbine engine.

The gasoline engine's favorable power-to-weight ratio enabled the early gyrating rotary-wing flying machines to get airborne vertically and sustain controlled hover and forward flight. Even Thomas A. Edison's genius couldn't solve the problems of vertical flight without sufficient power from a small, lightweight device. He even experimented with using electricity as the helicopter power plant, but it failed because of the problems associated with providing sufficient power to drive the electric motor. After a serious accident during the experiments, Edison proclaimed, "When an engine could be made that would weigh only three or four pounds to the horsepower, the problems of the air could be solved."[4] The Wright brothers were able to achieve sustained flight in their fixed-wing experimental aircraft on May 17, 1903 with a small lightweight reciprocating engine that weighed approximately thirteen pounds for each of the 12-hp it produced.

Igor Sikorsky's first helicopter design, built in 1909, utilized an Anzani 15-hp engine which was not sufficient to lift the coaxial-rotor craft off the ground. His second design, with a 25-hp Anzani, was able to lift its own weight of some four hundred pounds.[5] His famous VS-300A was able to maintain a sustained tethered hover flight on September 14, 1939, using a 90-hp Franklin radial engine. The weight of the aircraft was 1150 pounds. On May 13, 1940, it made its first untethered flight.

Refinements to the internal combustion engine had an even greater impact on rotary-wing aircraft development. The gas turbine engine with its significantly greater power-to-weight ratio compared to the heavier gasoline piston engine gave the helicopter designers what they needed to make the vertical flying machine not only fly better, lift more and perform longer, but also look better. The gas turbine engine enabled the helicopter to attain higher speeds, at which the aerodynamic shape of the fuselage had an impact on performance. Thus, the helicopters had to be streamlined. This greatly improved their visual appeal, as one can see by comparing the large-nosed Sikorsky H-34 to the relatively sleek gas turbine powered Bell UH-1 Huey.

The next important technological contribution that enhanced helicopter development was the refinement of the rotor system and flight control dynamics. During the experimental years of the 1920s and 1930s, helicopter design methods were relatively crude, with much of it done by trial and error. As the inventors and engineers learned more about the interplay of the complex aerodynamic forces involved, they were better able to find solutions to the problems. Over the years, a more scientific approach slowly replaced the costly trial and error method.

Nevertheless, there was one problem with helicopters that was, and still is, particularly difficult to deal with. Helicopters by their very nature are unstable, i.e, they do not want to fly, or remain on a chosen flight path by themselves, unlike fixed-wing aircraft which are designed to "want to fly" and, when trimmed properly, will continue on course and altitude unless interrupted by some outside force. The helicopter is very difficult to mechanically trim because of the wide variety of dynamic forces to which it is exposed.

There was no rest for the 1940's vintage helicopter pilot because he could not takes his hands off the controls for a moment—he literally had to fly his bucking machine every second the rotor blades were turning. In 1951, one student of helicopter aerodynamics described it this way:

> When the helicopter begins to hover the pilot's troubles start. For instance, ordinary air speed indicators go haywire below about 40 knots. The helicopter slips and slides around without regard to the movement of the immediate air mass. The attitude* of the fuselage of a fixed-wing plane more or less establishes the condition of flight. The reverse is true of the helicopter—the attitude of the fuselage follows the condition of flight.[6]

What this means is that in a fixed-wing aircraft, the pilot controls his aircraft by moving the various control surfaces on the wings, and it pretty much goes where the pilot tells it to go. On the other hand, the helicopter pilot essentially flies the rotor system; the fuselage, which is hanging from the rotors, goes where the rotor system takes it.

Many of the aerodynamic problems of stability, controllability and vibrations were "designed out" of helicopters with such innovations as the fully articulated rotor head** and rotor blade dampers. Many more of these problems have been solved partially by designing better dynamics and mostly by creating artificial stability. The latter method is achieved by interfacing sophisticated avionics and hydraulic flight control systems. This enables the helicopter's system to sense minute changes in the aircraft's attitude (which may be caused by wind gusts or air turbulence) and automatically apply subtle inputs into the hydraulic flight controls which are then transmitted to the rotor blades to stabilize flight. If a gust pitches the nose up, the automatic flight control system brings it back down to where it was without pilot intervention. While this is a very complex and a non-aerodynamic solution to helicopter stability, it does work.

Another important technological advancement leading to the acceptance of the helicopter as a combat vehicle was in the area of lightweight,

---

*Attitude refers to the position of the aircraft's fuselage in relation to the horizon. For example, when the nose of fuselage is pointing above the horizon, it is said to have a "nose high attitude."

**This rotor head design connects the rotor blades to the rotor hub in a way that allows the rotor blades to lead and lag and flap up and down as they spin during flight. This enhances stability and control, and minimizes vibration.

but powerful weapons. Armed helicopters have become a vital battlefield element in the last thirty years and will surely play an even greater role in the foreseeable future. Today, attack helicopters play an important role in just about every major military power's policy. Weapons technology, including target acquisition and fire control systems, is more a measure of helicopter tactical effectiveness than aeronautical engineering.[7]

The helicopters of the 1980s are being designed with particular combat scenarios in mind. In both conventional and guerrilla warfare, the helicopter has become essential because it can provide life saving, logistic, reconnaissance, close air support and fire suppression needs.

The attack helicopter is particularly well suited for employment in guerrilla warfare because it reduces the guerrilla's advantages. Typically, the guerrilla is native to the country and naturally adapted to it; he can move about and hide quickly because he knows the terrain. The helicopter reduces this advantage by increasing the counterinsurgent's mobility (so he can move quickly to "hot spots" with fresh forces without dependence on roads) and his ability to apply machine gun and rocket firepower quickly and accurately.

Even though the guerrilla knows the land, he is not spared the problems of rough terrain and adverse climatic conditions. Helicopters neutralize the terrain problem for the counterinsurgent and, in fact, give him a distinct advantage in this regard. In the desert, the problems of dust, intense heat, thirst, great distances and bright sun can take their toll. In cold climates, wind chill, blinding snow, rapidly changing weather, exposure, difficulty of movement, disease and low morale are less of a problem for the side that has heliborne support.

The attack helicopter is a force multiplier because the field commander is able to employ his forces with greater efficiency. In a mountainous region, the heavy helicopter saves the Army time and fatigue.[8] And with modern missile technology being applied to combat helicopters, the battle tank may become obsolete.

Armed helicopters also provide the field commander the means to move about the combat area for personal assessments. He is provided with aerial observations of the situation so he can deploy his forces more effectively. Visual intelligence of enemy strength and positions and a view of obstacles are vital to every battle plan. This can contribute to the vital element of surprise. Firepower and troops can be brought to the area quickly and with little warning. Helicopters also provide resupply and medevac in a way no other vehicle can.

Helicopters have changed the nature of modern warfare. The wars of the first half of the twentieth century moved at glacial speeds compared to today's. Ironically, while helicopters are a deadly force in combat, they are also responsible for saving more lives than previously possible. The wounded can be provided with almost immediate front-line medevac services. In fact, there are now helicopters designed specifically for combat rescue.

However long it took for helicopters to achieve acceptance and status in the minds of tacticians, it is unlikely that any military operation would be carried out today without them.

The Roots of Military Rotary-Wing Aviation

The Pioneers

The list of those who claim to be the first to do something that contributed to helicopter development is quite long. Many of the "firsts" are obscure, making them difficult, if not impossible, to prove.

The fabrication of a successful rotary-wing aircraft was a monumental achievement in aerodynamic design, engineering and construction. It required not only technical brilliance, but a lion's share of personal courage as well. At each stage there were many personal and financial risks involved for the developers.

Those who are indisputably major contributors to its design are as follows: the Italian, Leonardo da Vinci, who conceived of vertical flight in the year 1483 and made rough drawings of a rotary-type flying machine; the Russian, Mikhail V. Lomonosov, who built and flew a rotary-wing model in 1754; the Frenchmen, Louis and Jacques Breguet and Professor Charles Richet, who in 1907 constructed a full size rotary-wing flying machine able to lift itself and its pilot off the ground; the Spaniard, Juan de la Cierva, who built the first autogiro with an articulated rotor system in 1923; the Spanish-born Argentinean Marquess Raul Pateras Pescara, who built a flyable helicopter in 1925 with counter-rotating blades; and the Russian-born American, Igor Sikorsky, who on May 13, 1940 flew the practical helicopter for the first time in history. These unquestionably bold inventors deserve a place in history right beside the Wright brothers and Glen Curtiss. All of them had this in common: they knew their designs would not make it into the manufacturing stage without the support of the government, industry and the military.

Modern helicopter development was almost exclusively reserved for countries with strong economies and the will and the need to develop this valuable flying machine. Various governments showed early serious interest in developing rotary-wing aircraft. Because of the high costs and great risks involved in building these strange, new machines, they could not be reasonably supported by industry alone, especially as they had questionable commercial value. So, the governments of several nations helped promote and support early rotary-wing development, after which industry capitalized on the ideas and put them to commercial use.

United States Interest in Rotary-Wing Concepts

During the first decade of the twentieth century, the United States government took the initiative and decided to gamble on the helicopter with a small wager. On March 11, 1912 the secretary of the Navy authorized expenditures of less than $50 for developing models of a helicopter design proposed by Commodore F.E. Nelson of the USS *West Virginia.* The secretary's accompanying policy was followed with few exceptions for the next three decades. That is, the department recognized the value of the research to naval aviation and closely followed its development.[1] While merely a token commitment, it nevertheless stirred interest in the idea of aircraft that could fly vertically.

This interest spread to higher levels in the government during the next several years. On December 5, 1917, the secretaries of the War and Navy Departments established a policy on helicopter development based on the recomendations of the Joint Technical Board on Aircraft. The needs for improved power plants and propellers were recognized as necessary for the successful development of the helicopter. Actual support, however, was limited to moral encouragement until a vendor had demonstrated the value of the helicopter to the military.[2]

During these formative years, the thought of vertical flight was present but too risky to develop beyond models and experiments in the face of other aviation interests and national goals. Competition for support developed between fixed-wing and rotary-wing aircraft designers. Although attempts to build helicopters were being made in the early part of the century, the sudden success of fixed-wing flying from 1908 onward caused this kind of work to almost be abandoned.[3] Fixed-wing aircraft were already proven, and less complicated to design and build. The helicopter was an unproven concept that seemed too complex to deal with at the time. The fixed-wing flying machines seemed to be a better investment.

The Autogiro Emerges in Spain

During World War I, all aviation research was concentrated on fixed-wing aircraft. After the war was over, all but a few enthusiasts were convinced that there was no longer any point in developing rotating wings. Among those enthusiasts was Senor Don Juan de la Cierva, a Spanish inventor and airplane designer. The modern helicopter owes a great deal to his perseverance and technical ability.[4]

De la Cierva's efforts are considered to be some of the most significant technological breakthroughs toward the development of the true helicopter. His designs were so convincing, they were eventually tested in actual combat.

De la Cierva designed and built autogiros* during the early 1920s and gained international notoriety by doing so. After a lengthy period of working toward eliminating stall characteristics in airplanes, de la Cierva

*De la Cierva coined the trade name "autogiro" for his machines because the rotation of the blades was automatic. This word still has applications today such as in the term "autorotation." This unique feature of the helicopter allows it to land with no power by turning the rotor system during the descent by allowing the relative air movement to "windmill" the rotor. The mass of the turning rotors builds up inertia which can be utilized during the final phase of the approach to cushion the landing.

began building a ship utilizing wings that rotated around a central post.* He had learned that the lift principle operated in the same way on rotating wings as it did on fixed ones. At first de la Cierva tried using double rotors, one above the other, but the craft always wanted to turn over on its side. Then he discovered that if the rotor blades were flexible, this problem could be overcome.[5] Shortly afterward, on January 9, 1923, the first successful autogiro, de la Cierva's Model C.4, was flown at an airfield outside Madrid, Spain.** The plane made a complete circuit of approximately two and a half miles at an average speed of 37 miles per hour at an altitude of about eighty-two feet. This was the first officially observed flight of an autogiro—the first rotary-wing aircraft—and it drew considerable interest from military staffs in both Europe and the United States, which studied his designs to ascertain their military applications.

The autogiro, however, could not hover, which severely limited its prospective military uses. Nevertheless, it was the invention of the autogiro that swept away the fundamental problems that had beset a year-long attempt to devise a workable helicopter.[6] Accordingly, the lineage of rotary-wing aviation begins with the development of the autogiro, which essentially bridged the gap between the two distinctly different types of aircraft. That is, the autogiro was half fixed-wing and half rotary-wing.

The Military Interest in the Autogiro

The British government soon expressed curiosity about the autogiro for its possible military uses. In the summer of 1925 the British Air Ministry invited de la Cierva to give a series of demonstrations. If they proved his claims, he would be paid a substantial sum and receive an order for two aircraft.[7] By late October de la Cierva was ready for the tests which were set up to demonstrate his autogiro in various maneuvers, including a power-off, nearly-vertical descent from about fifteen hundred feet. For approximately four hours the tests were conducted for representatives of the government and the press until the aircraft was damaged during one of the high vertical landings.[8] The crash did not dampen the British interest in the autogiro. The Air Ministry ordered a number of de la Cierva's autogiros and they proved very useful in World War II as radar calibration aircraft and for School of Army Cooperation observer training. In 1932, the Cierva Flying School was created at Hamworth near London. The Chief Instructor was Mr. Alan March, a Royal Air Force Pilot. The Cierva school was thus the beginning of the Royal Air Force's rotary wing expertise.[9]

It wasn't until late in the 1920s that the United States began to take the autogiro seriously and study its potential for military service. Prior to 1929, most of the autogiro experiments had been conducted in Europe. It was time for the Americans to give it a try.

---

*De la Cierva's design resembled a biplane with the upper wing removed. In its place was a large, rotating propeller-like wing, mounted on a shaft in front of the cockpit. Cierva added a clutch between the front propeller and the rotating wing so that in taking off he could apply power for a few seconds to the rotating wing, thus pulling the machine upward as well as forward. Once aloft, the thrust generated by the forward propeller pulled the aircraft through the air, which forced the rotating wing to turn. This action, along with the lower wing, generated sufficient lift to stabilize flight.

**De la Cierva experimented with other successful autogiro configurations, one of which, the C.8, made the first rotary-wing aircraft English Channel crossing on September 18, 1928.

The vision of the development of vertical flight was shared on the other side of the Atlantic by Harold Pitcairn, an American entrepreneur and aviation pioneer. Dedicated to a lifetime search for a "safe airplane," Pitcairn traveled to England to see the de la Cierva Model C.8 up close. He was sufficiently impressed by what he saw. He learned to fly the C.8 and mastered its unique flying qualities. He bought it on the spot and brought it home for the American public to see. On December 18, 1928, the first Autogiro in America, a de la Cierva Model C.8, made its first flight with Pitcairn at the controls over his Bryn Athyn airfield, today the site of the Willow Grove Naval Air Station, near Philadelphia, Pennsylvania.[10]

The following February, at a cost of some $300,000, Harold Pitcairn purchased the U.S. rights to de la Cierva's autogiro. This eventually lead to the creation of two leading American autogiro companies: The Pitcairn Autogiro Company of America, Inc. and, licensed under it, the Kellett Autogiro Corporation. During this time, public interest in the potential of the autogiro was extremely high, and the Army Air Corps thought the autogiro would be useful for observation. Navy officers planned its role in submarine spotting and rescue work, and airlines saw the potential for an aerial taxi for their passengers.[11]

U.S. Navy's First Rotary-Wing Aircraft

The U.S. Navy bought its first autogiros on January 22, 1931, which included three XOP autogiros for flight tests from the Pitcairn Autogiro Company of America. The first of these craft, designated XOP-1, carried out service trials at Anacostia Field in Washington, D.C.,* and later at sea aboard the carrier *USS Langley;* the second was fitted with twin floats and the third was shipped to Nicaragua, where U.S. Marines were engaged in a counterinsurgency operation against guerrilla forces.[12]

Eight months and a day after they were purchased, on September 23, 1931, one of the Pitcairn autogiros, flown by Lieutenant (later Admiral) Alfred M. Pride, USN, made the first rotary-wing aircraft takeoffs and landings on a ship while underway—the *USS Langley*. Captain Kenneth Whiting, another naval aviation pioneer for whom the U.S. Navy's helicopter training base Naval Air Station Whiting in Milton, Florida is named, was aboard during this historic flight.

At the time, the autogiro was the only rotary-wing technology commercially available. From a military perspective, the major problems were that it had no immediate mission that could not be done by other types of aircraft and it had a very limited payload capacity. It did, however, have certain advantages that made it worth studying for possible use aboard ship and on the battlefield: It could take off and land in short distances and fly very slowly without stalling. Still, the U.S. Navy's evaluation of the autogiro in the early 1930s concluded that rotorplanes might be of some use in antisubmarine work when operated

*This field, located between what is now the South Capital Street Bridge and Bolling Airforce base, is presently used by VX-1, the U.S. Marine Corps Executive Support Detachment.

from auxiliaries, but that this appeared to be a minor application which hardly justified the expenditure of experimental funds.

U.S. Marine Corps Use the Autogiro in Nicaragua

In 1932, the third of the Navy's three Pitcairn XOP-1 autogiros was turned over to the Marine Corps for testing in competition with an O2U-1 Corsair biplane. The autogiro was taken by the Marines into active combat operations in Nicaragua that same year for what today would be called an operational evaluation. Gunnery Sergeant Harold Kaltenback, USMC, was directed to take the machine apart for shipment on the Navy transport USS *Vega* and reassemble it in Nicaragua.[13] When it arrived in Nicaragua, it was received by enthusiastic crowds, apparently because the Latin-American people took pride in the Spanish invention.[14] Its first flight, on June 27, 1932, received front page coverage in the Managuan newspaper *La Prensa.*

The tests of the XOP-1 were conducted throughout the summer of 1932 by three Marine pilots. The final report by the Marine pilots was sent to Marine Corps Headquarters in Washington, D.C. on November 22, 1932, by the commanding officer of the study group, Major Francis P. Mulcahy. The conclusion stated,

> It is the opinion (of the board) that the chief value the XOP-1 has on expeditionary duty is in landing to inspect small fields, whose value as landing areas has been recommended by ground troops, with a view to preparing these fields for other types; to evacuate medical sitting cases from landing areas that cannot be used by other types of planes; and to ferry important personnel to the same kind of landing area.[15]

The Marine involvement in Nicaragua ended on December 31, 1932, and the XOP-1 was once again dismantled by Sergeant Kaltenback for shipment back to Quantico, Virginia. There is little further mention of the XOP-1 in Marine records until November 6, 1933, when Captain Francis E. Pierce reported to Headquarters (after being detailed as artillery observer) to test the use of radiotelephony on an autogiro as a spotting platform for observation of the firing of 75 mm artillery. Pierce concluded that the autogiro was not satisfactory for artillery spotting due to its restricted field of vision and its relatively slow speed, which made it more susceptible to antiaircraft fire than the conventional airplane. The XOP-1 ended up crashing in 1934.[16]

The careers of the remaining two Navy Pitcairn autogiros also ended with disappointing results. One of them crashed for the second and last time in 1932. It was decided in August of that year that the last one should be put in storage. The Navy tried again in 1935 with a later model of the Pitcairn autogiro, the XOP-2, with the hope of obtaining a flying ambulance that could land on the deck of a battleship or cruiser if special provisions were made. But the new model was found unsatisfactory and even dangerous because of the vibration of the rotor. Two years later it was recommended the XOP-2 be flown to Norfolk for storage. Its only epitaph was a comment anonymously penciled in the margin of the recommendation: "Fly it, hell! Better crate the thing and ship it."[17]

First U.S. Army Tests of the Autogiro

The other autogiro manufacturer in the United States at the time was the Kellett Autogiro Corporation, founded in 1929 by two brothers, Wallace and Rod Kellett. They built several different models that looked much like the Pitcairn-Cierva designs. Most notably, a Kellett K-3 earned recognition by its use by Admiral Richard E. Byrd during his exploration of the Antarctic in 1933 and 1934.

The U.S. Army was given a Kellett KD-1A for evaluation in 1935 and the results were promising enough for additional purchases. In 1935 and 1936, the Air Corps obtained two Kellett YG-1A autogiros and an Pitcairn YG-2. These were used for test and evaluation purposes with rather unfortunate results: All three crashed and were destroyed in a short time. Since these test aircraft did not last long, the Air Corps did not get a complete picture of their military value.[18] Nevertheless, the War Department still believed there was something worthwhile in the autogiro, and allotted funds to procure seven more. The evaluations could be accelerated by having several planes, as the testing could be carried out concurrently by the Air Corps, the Artillery, the Infantry, the Coast Artillery and the Cavalry. The War Department stated that, if these test results warranted, more funds would be allotted for further development of the autogiro for military use.[19] As there was no commercial market for the autogiro at the time, manufacturers had to absorb development costs in the prices of their planes, and thus few manufacturers were interested. In fact, the Kellett Autogiro Company was the only firm that entered the competition, so the order was placed with it.

Each autogiro was estimated to cost the government between $40,000 and $50,000. To compare this to a fixed-wing aircraft at the time, a three-place observation plane cost approximately $30,000. Prior to this order, the Air Corps had already spent $450,000 on autogiros and their testing.

In 1938, the new Kellett YG-1B autogiros were delivered to Wright-Patterson Field in Dayton, Ohio, where the Air Corps had set up a training school for pilots and mechanics before the planes were sent out for in-service testing with ground elements of the Army.[20] The Kellett YG-1B was wingless and had a direct control design which used a pivotal three-bladed rotor. As an added feature, the blades of the rotors could be folded back over the tail. It was powered by one Jacobs R-755-3 engine, which was rated at 225-hp at 2000 rpm and was fitted with a Curtiss fixed-pitch metal propeller. The YG-1B had a top speed of 125 miles per hour and a cruising speed of 103 miles per hour This particular Kellett model could climb 1000 feet per minute, and had a range of 361 miles.

The first U.S. Army Air Corps autogiro training class graduated on May 21, 1938.

To the U.S. Army, the autogiro had demonstrated some military applications in their testing program. An obvious use was in directing artillery fire, as a successor to the old, unreliable observation balloon. Other possible applications were moving personnel around quickly over rough terrain or where roads were blocked by troops, evacuating the wounded and moving light equipment. Further tests involved aerial photography at low altitude and bombing missions.[21] However, even though the Army's testing lasted for several years, one after another the autogiro's supporters changed their minds.

War can have a strong influence on scientific and engineering development. Unfortunately, this was not the case with the autogiro. The time was not right for the autogiro's acceptance, either as a means of commercial transportation or as a military vehicle. Between World Wars I and II there was limited interest in studying the military potential of the autogiro. It was too difficult and expensive to build, rather hard to fly and unable to carry a suitable military payload.[22] The Air Corps began using light airplanes for many of the missions intended for the autogiro.

The Army eventually gave up on autogiros because of the many landing accidents and because too many tests were unsatisfactory. Lack of room and weight-lifting capacity were the chief objections to the Kellett as well as the Pitcairn models.[23] Also, the true helicopter was showing promise with Louis Breguet's Gyroplane Laboratoire which flew for the first time on June 26, 1933.*

This chapter in the story of the autogiro has a tragic footnote. On December 9, 1936, de la Cierva was killed in the crash of a Dutch airliner at Croydon, England. He had devoted his life to developing safe aircraft that would not stall, and he lost it in a plane that crashed on takeoff.

The autogiro was a remarkable aircraft with many capabilities, but it was a flying machine without a mission. Had weapons systems been as refined as they are today, the autogiro idea might have taken root. As it was, "off the shelf" models were tested to see if they were fit for military duty. If initial tests had been performed to determine possible operational applications, specifications for a better autogiro might have been developed. It seems obvious that there was little real interest in the development of this ingenious aircraft, which the Nicaraguan newspapers unfairly dubbed the "turkey hen."[24]

---

*The Brequet helicopter had two-bladed, counter-rotating coaxial rotors and was powered by a 350-hp Hispano 9Q engine. It was capable of vertical (collective) and horizontal (cyclic) control and set several world records.

World War II Rotary-Wing Aircraft

The outbreak of World War II was the unfortunate catalyst that accelerated the development of rotary-wing aircraft. The lesson learned before World War II was that the autogiro proved to be too limited for combat because of its insufficient payload capacity and its inability to take off and land vertically. A vehicle that could get airborne without a rolling start and carry a reasonable payload was what the military planners wanted. The true helicopter was the only answer. This type of machine, however, was still in experimental stages when the autogiro was already in production.

Only the nations with the essential engineering expertise could design and build this radically new type of flying machine. A strong industry, wealth available for investment, technical expertise, the interest of inventors and, perhaps most importantly, the will of a dedicated group of pioneers are what made the difference.

The French military had become intrigued with the helicopter designed by a gifted Argentinean name Raul Pateras de Pescara in Barcelona, Spain. During the early stages of its development in 1921, a French military commission traveled to Barcelona for the first official military trials of Pescara's helicopter. This commission, which included the widely known aviator de Romanet, announced to the press, "We have found Pescara's helicopter admirably constructed (and) so good that it may be stated that the present machine gives promise of much greater chances of success than any that have been hitherto designed."[1] In 1922, Pescara went to France where he received support in the form of funds from the Service Technique de L'Aeronautique. With this encouragement, he constructed a second coaxial-rotor helicopter which demonstrated remarkable control and flying characteristics. His designs showed great insight with the ability to change the pitch of the blades while in flight for maneuverability and the unique feature of autorotation.

The German Helicopter Experience

By most accounts, the first practical helicopter was flown on June 26, 1936 in Germany. It was a curious looking rotorcraft called the Focke-

Achgelis Fa61, designed and built by Dr. Heinrich Karl Johann Focke for the Third Reich, even though he had been displaced by the Nazis as being "politically unsafe."[2] He had established his own company, Focke-Achgelis, to design and build helicopters and autogiros under a license agreement with de la Cierva.

His Fa 61 was a single-seat aircraft with twin side-by-side three-bladed rotors. It was constructed from a variety of other airframe parts with certain components from Weir of Scotland and the fuselage of the Fw 44 Stieglitz. Most of the forward thrust was provided by a forward-facing 160-hp propeller engine, which also provided power to the rotor systems.

It was a difficult aircraft to fly; even Germany's crack test pilot Karl Franke only agreed to one tethered trial. There was one pilot available who seemed to possess a natural ability to fly virtually any type of aircraft, including the helicopter. The Fa 61, piloted by Flugkapitän Hanna Reitsch,* made spectacular demonstrations on numerous occasions, most notably flying in the Berlin Deutschlandhall sports arena in February 1938. One account says that because of its remarkable handling characteristics and freedom, Reitsch called it "intoxicating."

Later, the Fa 61 demonstrated its ability to fly long distances at reasonable speeds by flying cross-country from Bremen to Berlin at an average speed of 75 miles per hour. In other tests, it reached an altitude of 11,700 feet.[3]

Not long after Focke demonstrated the reliability of his Fa 61 during the late 1930s, President Franklin D. Roosevelt requested and obtained funds for the development of a similar craft for the United States.[4] But, military aviation was changing during the late 1930s and the timing was wrong for rapid acceptance. Fixed-wing aircraft dominated during this period and helicopter aviation was almost considered a curious novelty. This was essentially caused by the military application failures of the autogiro.

Between 1936 and 1938, Dr. Focke proved that the helicopter could be a very practical air vehicle, although he did not intend for his designs to be used for military purposes. The Nazis, however, had different plans.

Another German helicopter pioneer that helped shape the course of the use of rotary-wing aircraft in combat was Anton Flettner. Starting as early as 1922 with helicopter experiments, he was the first to use intermeshing, counter-rotating synchronized rotors, which were subsequently adopted by Kamov and Kaman.[5]

In 1942 Flettner's highly successful twin-bladed, twin-rotor F1 282 Kolibri two-seat helicopter, which was flown for the first time in 1940, was operational on German warships and escorts in the Mediterranean, Baltic and Aegean Seas. This remarkable helicopter is considered by many to be the world's first military helicopter. A later version was used for antisubmarine warfare.

---

*Hanna Reitsch was a gifted aviator and one of Germany's most respected test pilots. She was born in Hirschberg in 1914 and died in 1979.

Early Luftwaffe Interest in Vertical Lift

The Fa 61 was the first helicopter of any nation to be formally registered. The prototypes were assigned German registrations D-EBVU and D-EKRA. From 1937 to 1939, the Fa 61 established several helicopter flight records, among them a speed of 77 miles per hour, a distance of 143 miles and an altitude of 11,243 feet.

The next Focke creation was the much larger Fa 233 Drache, the world's first transport helicopter.[6] It was essentially a larger version of the Fa 61 and had considerable potential military applications. It was a six-passenger aircraft with a 1000-hp engine configured in the center of its steel tube and fabric fuselage. While under construction at the Laupheim factory, seven survived several Allied bombing raids. These were the only Fa 233 helicopters to be completed at Laupheim. On June 21, 1943, the first Fa 233 completed at Laupheim, the V11, was flown by Karl Bode for a series of films in which a variety of heavy external loads were demonstrated.[7]

Because it showed great promise for operating in mountainous terrain, it was decided to test the Fa 233 as a general-purpose transport for troops at the Mountain Warfare School in Mittenwalde, a small resort town in the mountains near Innsbruck. The commanding officer of the School, Oberst Kraitmeyer, selected mountain landing sites in the light of possible battle scenarios. Karl Bode participated as the works pilot on behalf of Focke-Achgelis, along with two Luftwaffe pilots: Lieutenant Gerstenhouer and Unteroffizier Lex. A typical operation during these trials consisted of a light mountain gun and ammunition being transported by cargo net to a site some 5900 feet (1800 m) below the Wornergrant peak from where it was then recovered and carried at the end of a fifty-two foot (16 m) cable to a higher location beneath the Grat where it was not possible to land. This series of mountain trials, completed on October 5, 1944, would undoubtedly have contributed much to helicopter development under other circumstances.

An unexpected order was issued on October 11, 1944, forbidding the further testing of the Fa 233 and sending Focke-Achgelis personnel to the Messerschmitt. Characteristic of the confusion that then permeated Berlin, a short time later not only was flight testing resumed, but the Focke-Achgelis organization was ordered to reassemble at Berlin's Tempelhof Airport and to prepare to manufacture the Fa 233 at a rate of four hundred per month! Such an order was totally unrealistic at that point in the European conflict. Apart from sufficient machines, jigs, tools and materials, which were not available, such prodigious production would have demanded a labor force equivalent to the populace of a medium-sized town.[8]

In late 1944, there were only five Fa 233 helicopters still operational. The V12, which was ultimately lost while attempting to rescue seventeen people from a snowcapped mountain, had been proposed by SS-Hauptsturmführer Otto Skorzeny to be used to rescue Benito Mussolini from imprisonment in the hotel at the peak of the Gran Sasso Massif in the Abruzzi e Molise region, northeast of Rome, in September 1943. However, the Fa 233 became unserviceable at the last moment and, with no other helicopter available, the use of the Fi 156 Storch was necessitated.[9]

The First and Only World War II Luftwaffe Helicopter Squadron

The three surviving Drache helicopters were assigned to the first and only true Luftwaffe helicopter squadron, Transportstaffel Forty, established in 1945 at Mühldorf, Bavaria, and commanded by Hauptmann Josef Stangl.[10] At about the same time, Focke-Achgelis had succeeded in resuming production of the Drache at its new facilities at Tempelhof. This spawned the first new Fa 233 (Werke-Nr 00051), coded GW+PA, accepted by the Luftwaffe and immediately assigned by "Order of the Führer" to fly to Danzig, in northern Poland, on the night of February 25, 1945. The reason for the flight was never made known, but it was probably to try to effect an escape of Gauleiter Karl Hanke from the besieged City of Breslau.[11]

Meanwhile, the Allies began closing in and threatening the helicopter assets. The advance of the United States Eightieth Infantry Division over the Pyhrnpass in the direction of Liezen early in May forced the Staffel to move westward along the River Enns to Radstadt at the foot of the Alps. From here, Hauptmann Stangl tried to retreat, only to be taken prisoner by U.S. forces near Salzburg. Only two Fa 233s succeeded in reaching Ainring, which were also captured by the United States' forces.

Thus, the wartime career of the Drache came to a somewhat ignominious end. Three more Fa 233s were nearly completed at Tempelhof, with about fifteen more in various stages of assembly. These all fell into the hands of the Soviets. Not more than eleven examples of this epoch-making helicopter, including the prototypes, were completed and flown, but these had accumulated some four hundred hours of flight time and about six thousand miles of cross-country flying. Some thirty-seven other Drache helicopters had reached advanced stages of assembly, and component parts equivalent to about twenty additional helicopters had been manufactured in the three factories occupied by the Focke-Achgelis concern during its eight years of existence.[12]

The German Rotary-Wing Kite

An ingenious, although questionable, rotary-wing aircraft designed, built and used by the Germans during World War II was known as the Focke-Achgelis Fa 330 Rotary-Wing Kite. This unusual aircraft was an engineless, three-bladed rotating-type kite that operated on the autogiro principle. It was used as an elevated observation platform for one man.

The kite became airborne by being towed from a submarine deck to which it was attached by a steel cable working from a winch.[13] It was designed to be folded and stowed aboard the submarine and deployed rapidly soon after it surfaced. The observer communicated with the U-boat captain via a direct-connect telephone. Some two hundred of these Fa 330s were built and flown by enlisted submarine personnel.[14]

Post-War Allied Interest in Focke Helicopters

Following World War II, France, England and the United States all wanted Focke's expertise. France won the dispute with the United Kingdom and the United States as to who should have the services of Heinrich Focke. He and twelve of his principal technicians were taken to France to work for the Societe Nationale de Constructions Aeronautiques du Sud-Est (SNCASE) at the initiative of Colonel Garry of the Service Technique de l'Aeronautique. There they began to restore many of the drawings of the Fa 233 which had been partially burned by French troops.[15] The first Fa 233 was completed and designated SE 3000 No. 1 and registered F-WFDR. It flew on October 23, 1948, piloted by Henri Stakenburg, accompanied by another test pilot, Jean Boulet and a mechanic, Marcel Hochet.* Three more SE 3000s were built but had a variety of technical problems.

After the war, two intact Fa 233s were captured at Ainring. An agreement was eventually reached that one of these, Fa 233 V14, would be sent to United Kingdom. This helicopter, which had logged some 170 hours in the air since its first flight in July 1943, had flown more than any helicopter in the world at that time. During its ferry flight to the Royal Air Force's Experimental Establishment at Beaulieu on July 25, 1945, it made the first helicopter crossing of the English Channel.[16] Unfortunately, it crashed during a test flight in the United Kingdom on October 3, 1945.

The Focke design was a clever addition to helicopter technology. A variation of this side-by-side rotor system was developed in the United States by Frank Piasecki, who observed and flew in the French SE 3000. This new design took the form of the tandem rotor configuration; that is, the rotors were mounted at each end of the fuselage rather than on each side. Today, this configuration is seen on the Boeing CH-46 Sea Knight and the CH-47 Chinook.

These events signal the end of what might be considered the beginning chapter in the story of the practical helicopter. The end of World War II brought with it optimistic forecasts of the widespread introduction of the helicopter in both civil and military aviation. In the early post-war years there were innumerable helicopter designs and projects under way, but 'helicoptering' was young in practice if old in theory, and it was to be a long time before other helicopter designers were to successfully emulate

*Both Strakenburg and Boulet had participated in helicopter flying courses in the USA. Strakenburg was a French citizen. He had been the test pilot of the SNCASE's rotary wing division for some years flying the Cierva-licensed Leo C 30 Autogiro and its derivatives, the Leo C 301 and C 302. *Air International,* June 1984, page 295.

the numerous achievements of Henrick Focke. It was said that the helicopter symbolized the victory of ingenuity over common sense.[17]

U.S. Military Interest in Early Helicopters

Meanwhile, in the United States, a U.S. Army captain named H. Frank Gregory observed Igor Sikorsky's experiments and flight demonstrations of the VS-300 prototype in 1940. He then took a rather dramatic step and recommended to the Army Air Corps that Sikorsky be contracted to build a helicopter for operational use, in spite of the failures of the autogiros.[18]

At the same time, interest in helicopters was growing enough for the Sikorsky Aircraft Aviation Corporation to become a subsidiary of United Aircraft (as United Technologies was then known). The Chance Vought and Sikorsky divisions were combined during the development of the VS-300 (the "VS" designation stood for Vought and Sikorsky). In 1943, Sikorsky Aircraft became a separate division, totally dedicated to helicopter production.

In January 1941, flight testing of the VS-300 was resumed, and the U.S. Army Air Corps issued a contract to Sikorsky Aircraft to build a two-place observation helicopter to be powered by a 160-hp Warner engine.[19] The contract amounted to $50,000 for the XR-4 prototype. The XR-4 flew for the first time on January 14, 1942. This was the first helicopter built for military purposes. On the day of its maiden flight, Sikorsky was so sure of his new design he flew six test flights. The following April at Stratford, Connecticut, it was flown for a gathering of United States and British military officials, impressively demonstating its stability and maneuverability.

Further proof of the maturity of this new technology was given when the XR-4 departed on its delivery flight of some 760 miles from Stratford, Connecticut, to Wright Field, in Dayton, Ohio. This flight was made without any problems, in spite of widely-varying weather conditions. When the XR-4 arrived on May 17, 1942, it had broken practically all existing helicopter records.[20]

Sikorsky had proven that America had the technology and the know-how to build a reliable helicopter. This sparked interest in military utilization of the helicopter on both sides of the Atlantic. In May, 1943, tests were conducted in conjunction with the Army Air Corps, the War Shipping Administration and the Coast Guard to prove the capability of the YR-4 to operate from the deck of a ship.

Helicopters enjoyed a surge of curiosity in the United States during 1942 and 1943, probably due to their greater capabilities when compared to the less than desirable autogiro. The momentum of the interest in the favorable results with the Sikorsky helicopters was enough for the armed forces to begin taking these strange aircraft seriously.

On July 24, 1942, the U.S. Navy Bureau of Aeronautics issued a planning directive calling for the procurement of four Sikorsky helicopters for study and development by the Navy and Coast Guard aviation forces.[21] This is essentially the birthday of U.S. Naval helicopter aviation.

In 1943, the orders for Sikorsky helicopters began pouring in. The R-5, a larger and much improved design, took off for the first time on August 18, 1943, and the R-6 on October 15, 1943. More than four hundred of these three models were built for military use in World War II. They saw service with the U.S. Army, the U.S. Navy, the U.S. Coast Guard, the British Navy and the British Air Force.

In the U.S. Navy, the helicopter's flexibility of operation and its ability to land and take off in small spaces meant that it could operate successfully from cruisers and battleships as well as carriers. It made a good scout, and was able to relieve destroyers of some of the numerous mail-delivering duties as well as the duty of plane guard in carrier operations.[22]

So, this interest was not unfounded. There was also a growing submarine threat and every available asset was being examined to deal with the problem. Finally, helicopters had a bonafide mission that gave them the credibility needed to be included in fleet operations.

Winston Churchill summed up the submarine menace during World War II as, "The only thing that ever really frightened me during the war."[23] It was not surprising that fleet commanders were becoming more convinced of the possible use of the helicopter in the antisubmarine warfare role. Several Coast Guard officers witnessed flight demonstrations of the Sikorsky XR-4 and recognized its potential for these duties. It seemed particularly suited to protect convoys against submarine attack, which was one of the major concerns in the United States and Great Britain.[24] They were convinced that the helicopter could be put to good use in this type of warfare.

The time was right: not only was a bonafide combat mission waiting for helicopters, but the right man was in a position to listen to their proposals. The Chief of Naval Operations, Admiral Ernest J. King, was a strong believer in the value of convoy operations who once wrote, "Escort is not just one way of handling the submarine menace, it is the only way that gives any promise of success."[25] Accordingly, he supported the proposal of the Coast Guard officers. The commander in chief of the U.S. fleet assigned responsibility for sea-going development of helicopters and their operation in convoys to the Coast Guard on February 15, 1943. It was also directed that tests be carried out to determine if helicopters operating from merchant ships would be of value in combating submarines.[26] This was followed on May 4, 1943, by a second directive from the commander, to expedite the evaluation of the helicopter in antisubmarine operations and to form a "joint board" with representatives of the commander in chief of the U.S. fleet, the Bureau of Aeronautics, the Coast Guard, the British Admiralty and the Royal Air

Force. The resulting Combined Board for the Evaluation of the Ship-Based Helicopter in Antisubmarine Warfare was later expanded to include representatives of the Army Air Force, the War Shipping Administration and the National Advisory Committee for Aeronautics.[27]

On May 7, 1943, Navy representatives witnessed landing trials of the XR-4 (HNS-1 Navy designation) helicopter aboard the merchant tanker *Bunker Hill* in a demonstration conducted in Long Island Sound sponsored by the Maritime Commission. The pilot, Colonel H. Frank Gregory, USA Air Corps, made some fifteen flights, during which he landed on the water before returning to the platform on the deck of the ship.[28] Takeoffs and landings were accomplished from the tanker from amidships between the pilot house and the mast, the only relatively clear area.[29]

Lieutenant Commander Frank A. Erickson, USCG, the first Coast Guard helicopter pilot, accepted the Navy's first helicopter, a Sikorsky HNS-1 (identical to the Army's R-4) in October 1943 and set up shop at Naval Air Station Brooklyn. His unit's first responsibility was learning how to maintain and fly helicopters, then teaching others from all the services. The unit also set about developing the rescue hoist, the autopilot, instrument and night flying capability, a loud speaker and other necessary hardware as well as rescue techniques.[30]

On December 18, 1943, based on his belief that tests indicated the practicability of ship-based helicopters, the chief of naval operations separated pilot training from test and development. He further directed that, effective January 1, 1944, a helicopter pilot training program was to be conducted by the U.S. Coast Guard at Floyd Bennett Field under the direction of the deputy, chief of naval (air) operations. [31]

Because of its growing versatility, the helicopter saw early development in the field of medical evacuation. On December 20, 1943, Lieutenant Commander Erickson reported that the Coast Guard Air Station at Floyd Bennett Field had experimented with a helicopter used as an airborne ambulance. An HNS-1 helicopter made flights carrying, in addition to its normal crew of a pilot and a mechanic, a weight of two hundred pounds in a stretcher suspended approximately four feet beneath the twin floats. In further demonstrations during the following year, the stretcher was attached to the side of the fuselage and landings were made at the steps of the dispensary.[32] It is ironic that even though the U.S. Coast Guard was the first to begin testing the helicopter as an air ambulance, it was a civilian—Dimitry "Jimmey" Viner, Sikorsky's chief test pilot—who made the first actual rescue in an Army helicopter with a Coast Guard rescue hoist on November 29, 1945. A Coast Guard helicopter and pilot made the first rescues of carrier pilots by a "plane guard" helicopter while deployed with the USS *Midway* in March 1946. The HNS-1 was piloted by Lieutenant Walter C. Bolton, USCG, and the mission was carried out in sub-zero temperatures during Operation Frostbite.[33]

One significant series of tests was conducted to study the adaptability of helicopters to ships operating at sea. On January 16, 1944 Lieutenant Junior Grade S.R. Graham, USCG, was en route from New York to Liverpool on the British freighter *Daghestan,* which was carrying some eight thousand tons of grain and two R-4B (HNS-1) helicopters. Weather conditions prevented any flight operations before the tenth day out. Then, in mid-Atlantic, with the ship still rolling from ten to fifteen degrees and the deck heaving from ten to twenty feet, Graham took off in a 20 knot wind without difficulty and flew around the convoy for thirty minutes. It took several attempts, but he managed to land safely.[34] Weather during the mid-winter crossing of the North Atlantic allowed only two other flights, and so the sponsoring Combined Board for Evaluation of the Ship-based Helicopter in Anti-Submarine Warfare concluded that the helicopter's capability should be developed in coastal waters until models with improved performance became available.[35]

Airborne Medevac

Medical evacuation by aircraft found its roots in the imaginations of two young U.S. Army officers just after the turn of the century. The first known aircraft equipped for the transport of patients appeared in 1910. Captain George H.R. Cosman and Lieutenant A.L. Rhoades of Fort Barrancas, Florida, modified (at their own expense) and flew an aeroplane for transporting patients.[36] Their ingenuity was not fully appreciated at the time, and their efforts generated little interest.

It was only after the United States entered World War I that the airborne medevac concept was officially used. During World War I the airplane was used sporadically to evacuate patients. In 1918, Major Nelson E. Driver of the Medical Corps, and Captain William C. Ocker of the Air Service converted a JN-4 (Jenny) airplane into an ambulance. This was used primarily for the return of patients from aircraft accidents.[37]

Fixed-wing aircraft had obvious limitations in the environment of the battlefield, and so much attention was given to the possible uses of rotary-wing aircraft. The Field Medical Service School at Carlisle Barracks in Pennsylvania had experimented with aircraft for use in patient evacuation. In 1936, it field-tested an autogiro as a forward evacuation vehicle. The idea was discarded, but for engineering and budgetary considerations rather than any defect in the basic concept.[38] The lack of funds, however, did not halt the interest in or the realization of the need for medevac on the battlefield.

U.S.Army Experiments with Heliborne Medevac

On the other side of the world, during the mid-1940s, rotary-wing aviation saw some of its earliest operational use. The British government had purchased a number of Sikorsky R-4 helicopters, four of which eventually reached the China-Burma-India theater. Here the first known use of the helicopter for medical evacuation occurred; certainly it was the first from behind enemy lines.

It happened in April 1944 during Britain's advance to recapture Burma from the Japanese when a light airplane carrying three casualties was forced down behind enemy lines.[39] The pilot and the casualties were not injured. A message was dropped to the group directing them to burn their aircraft and climb a nearby ridge, where food and supplies were dropped. Realizing it would be impossible to rescue the group by airplane, Colonel Philip Cochran, USA, called upon his helicopters.* An R-4 was sent from Lalukhet to Taro, India, a base for light plane operations in North Burma. At Taro the R-4 was fitted with an L-5 gasoline tank and then flown non-stop across the mountains to a base about twenty five miles from the downed group. Another message was dropped to instruct the group to make their way to a rice paddy. There the helicopter rescued them one by one. Thereafter the R-4 was placed in regular use as a medical evacuation vehicle in that area, and in the next several days, eighteen more missions were flown.[40] This led to daily flights to evacuate casualties from columns fighting in north central Burma.

Rescue in the jungles of Burma was extremely difficult to carry out on foot because of the thick undergrowth and the lack of roads.

> For that reason it became increasingly important to provide effective rescue in order to bolster the morale of the air crews. L-1B's and L-5s (fixed-wing aircraft) were brought in, as they were the only aircraft available which could even be considered for use in the jungle. They were successful in a few instances where small clearings could be found, but the vast majority of cases required a walk-out, which caused the death of many allied personnel, who, despite all efforts, could not be trained effectively to survive in the jungle.[41]

The United States Army continued to realize the benefits of heliborne medevac in the jungles and mountains of Burma and the positive impact it had on the troops. On January 17, 1945, General George E. Stratemyer, commander of the forces at the time, sent a letter to Washington stating simply that he badly needed helicopters. At the time, five of his pilots were down and his equipment did not allow their removal. He asked that six helicopters be shipped as soon as possible to form an emergency squadron which was to consist of three flights, each with two YR-5s or YR-6s, fifteen officers, and thirty-five enlisted members. Authorization for the helicopters was granted even though they were still in the experimental stages. Without delay they were disassembled and shipped in replacement cargo aircraft.

Sikorsky R-4 helicopters were first used for rescue by the U.S. Army Air Forces in Burma and India in the spring of 1945. Before the end of the war, Sikorsky R-6 helicopters were also being used by a rescue organization in China, but rescue units elsewhere were not equipped with helicopters until after V-J Day.[42]

---

*Colonel Cochran was the commander of the United States' First Air Commando Group, which was based at Hailakandi, India.

During clean-up operations immediately after the war, better helicopters were brought in to help. The development of the R-5 and R-6 helicopters made more powerful machines available, and in April 1945, five R-6s were sent to China (by this time, air emphasis had shifted to the Hump and China, as Burma had been freed). These helicopters were accompanied by four helicopter mechanics and one trained Sikorsky troubleshooter. The R-6s had been crated and stowed inside C-47s, which flew them to China along with seven thousand pounds of spare parts. These parts were to insure adequate supply for at least the first six months of operation.[43] This technique of disassembling helicopters for transportation in fixed-wing logistics aircraft to in-theater areas is still used routinely today.

Once in the theater, it was found that operations would start from a field 6250 feet above sea level, a higher base than had ever been used for helicopters. One of the helicopters was taken out of a C-47 and assembled in twenty hours. It was flown successfully one afternoon in May 1945 with two men and two and one-half hours worth of gas for fifteen minutes. During the following week the remaining four helicopters, two of which had been ferried over the Hump by the C-47s and the two that had been flown over by C-54s, were assembled and flown.[44]

Extensive testing during this time proved the operational capabilities of these fragile flying machines. The helicopters were flown with comparative ease at 13,500 feet, and vertical takeoffs (zero runs) were made from as high as 7200 feet. A helicopter was flown for five hours with a reserve of one-half hour's gasoline—an unofficial world's endurance record. It was able to hover as high as twenty feet above the ground at 6500 feet above sea level. With two men and a full load of gas, and at economical pitch setting, it would indicate 75 miles per hour at seven thousand feet, burning twelve gallons of gas an hour. This gave a range of four hundred miles. This range was increased to six hundred miles by a combination of extra fuel tanks and increased seating capacity.[45]

The first U.S. Army Air Corps helicopter rescue in China took place on May 28, 1945, and it proved the importance of helicopter medevac. Three Americans were found in a valley in the heart of the Hump, completely isolated from American bases. The only way of getting them out, prior to the arrival of the helicopters in China, was a walk-out, which would have required two to three weeks, at least. Three helicopters were flown in from the nearest staging areas, made the pick-up and flew the men back to safety, a one way trip which required one hour and twenty minutes .[46]

Many lessons were learned from these early operations which fueled the Army's interest in helicopters. From the experience of operating helicopters in Burma and China, it was determined that the R-6, with modifications, would accommodate two people and one hundred gallons of gas, or four people and fifty gallons of gas, and, with a winch, was capable of providing complete rescue coverage within a three hundred mile radius of its operating base anywhere in the world, except, perhaps, in portions of the Andes and Tibetan plateaus.[47]

Near the end of World War II the U.S. Army's interest in the helicopter increased. Early in 1945 the Army began investigating the feasibility of adapting rotary-wing aircraft to the aviation mission. The first Army helicopter pilots were trained in late 1945 under an informal agreement with the Army Air Corps. They were selected individually and trained in Sikorsky R-4 and R-6 helicopters at Scott Field, Illinois and Sheppard Field, Texas.[48]

The following year, the Bell Helicopter Company was contracted to train pilots and mechanics. This was the beginning of a long and fruitful relationship between this company and the Army. Bell Aircraft Corporation, then in Buffalo, New York, had begun in 1941 developing a small utility helicopter that would become one of the longest serving helicopters in history. This versatile machine employed a unique rotor system design using only two rotor blades. It was designated the YR-13, and was first flown on December 8, 1945. Variants of the YR-13 are still flying today. Its designations have included the H-13 Sioux, the HUL, the HTL, and the Scout.

In early 1946, the U.S. Army purchased thirteen Bell H-13s for testing by the Army Field Forces Board Number One and the Eighty-Third Airborne Division at Fort Bragg, North Carolina and the Second Infantry Division at Fort Lewis, Washington. Early the following year, the Army Air Corps agreed to conduct helicopter primary training at Randolph Field Sub Base in San Marcos, Texas. The first class convened in September with four students flying the YR-13. Formal helicopter advanced tactical training began in October 1948 at Fort Sill, Oklahoma. The Army Aviation School was moved to Fort Rucker, Alabama in 1954, where it remains today.[49]

Emergency Helicopter Combat Operations

Jungle medevac was the beginning of the operational use of helicopters in the lifesaving role. The dramatic rescue in Burma resulted in the regular use of the R-4 for medical evacuation. Other R-4s were eventually used in the Philippines. There, in the latter stages of the campaign, the Thirty-Eighth Infantry Division used them to evacuate mountain positions. This eliminated the need for dangerous and tiring stretcher-bearing.[50] No longer did the U.S. Army have to rely entirely on wheeled vehicles to reach remote positions or carry their wounded out of jungle battlegrounds.

In the United States, another type of mission was performed that demonstrated not only the versatility of the helicopter, but also its reliability in adverse weather conditions. On January 3, 1944 a helicopter mercy mission was carried out by Commander Frank A. Erickson, USCG, flying an HNS-1 helicopter. He made an emergency delivery of forty units of blood plasma from lower Manhattan Island to Sandy Hook, New York, where the plasma was administered to survivors of an explosion on the destroyer USS *Turner*. The flight was made through snow and sleet, which had grounded all other types of aircraft.[51]

The first U.S. naval aviator to perform a bonafide helicopter rescue occurred the following year. It was a Coast Guard pilot. On May 2, 1945 Lieutenant August Kleisch, USCG, flying a HNS-1 helicopter rescued eleven Canadian airmen who were stranded in northern Labrador about 125 miles from Goose Bay.[52]

Helicopters On Sea Duty

The Navy conducted numerous experiments during the 1940s to test the compatibility of helicopters with shipboard missions. The first cruise aboard a carrier was made in March 1946 with a Coast Guard HNS-1 and a Coast Guard pilot. Lieutenant Walter C. Bolton was assigned to the carrier *Midway*, the flagship of Operation Frostbite, to test the worthiness of the craft for air-sea rescue duty and scouting during carrier operations conducted in sub-zero temperatures and high winds in the Arctic.

Although no rescues were attempted during this operation, the potential for use of the helicopter was recognized by the Chief of the Bureau of Aeronautics, Rear Admiral H.B. Sallada, who said, "The ability to hover above a surface and lower a hoist to (a downed pilot) without landing is a definite asset as compared to the light seaplane which can operate only on a moderate sea."[53] The Navy later bought three of the first five HOS-1s.

Antisubmarine Development

The Germans spearheaded the use of helicopters against submarines as early as 1944 during World War II with the highly reliable Flettner Fl 285, an Antisumarine Warfare (ASW) version of the Flettner Fl 282. This remarkable helicopter was assigned to various German ships and escorts and was equipped with two small depth charges. A highly capable helicopter, it was used extensively during the latter phases of the war for sub hunting and aerial reconnaissance. It was also configured with a cabling device so that it could be winched down to the deck during landings in rough sea conditions. This was very likely the earliest version of what is known today in the U.S. Navy as light helicopter antisubmarine (HSL) warfare squadrons, i.e., a light helicopter assigned to small ASW ships for spotting, light logistics and ASW operations.

In the mid-1940s, with the development of a dipping sonar, the U.S. Navy became very interested in the possible use of helicopters for sub hunting.

Invented by Dr. H.C. Hayes of the Naval Research Laboratory (NRL), the dipping sonar was originally designed for use from blimps in antisubmarine warfare but was later redesigned for helicopter installation. After extensive development and laboratory testing, the Hayes Submarine Sound Equipment was installed in an XHOS helicopter for an at-sea evaluation. The test program began on February 14, 1945, with the XHOS operating from the Coast Guard cutter *Cobb* off Block Island. An actual submarine was used as a target. Commander F.A. Erickson and Lieutenant Junior Grade Stewart Graham of the Coast Guard took turns piloting the helicopter with civilians Coop and Rather of the NRL alternating as sonar operators.[54]

Successful ASW tests with helicopters continued with much being accomplished in early 1946 at the Naval Research Laboratory. This time it was with an improved version of the dipping sonar gear, now designated the XCF sonar. The Coast Guard had just taken delivery of one of two HO2S's, so installation began immediately.

In March 1946 Project Pilot Graham and his mechanic flew the HO2S to Key West for temporary duty with the ASW Development Squadron VX-1. This time the trials were against a German Type XXI submarine, the most modern sub afloat. Unfortunately, the tests had to be terminated after three months when the overloaded HO2S did not have sufficient power to hover on a hot humid day while trying to land aboard a Landing Ship Transport (LST) and crashed into the water.[55]

This slowed VX-1 dipping sonar experiments for a few years, but in 1950 they resumed, using the more capable tandem-rotor Piasecki HRP-1 Rescuer in testing the new AN/AQS-4 sonar. The squadron maximized its hover performance by stripping the steel tube fuselage of its fabric covering. The gain in lift was greater than the net reduction in weight because the download on the fuselage was also reduced. The tandem rotor concept was preferred because of its superior hovering ability and center of gravity range compared to the single rotor helicopter. Therefore, the Piasecki HUP-2 was ordered and developed as the interim ASW helicopter. Before the HUP-2 could be delivered, however, they became the victims of chronic engine problems.[56]

The successes of these early experiments set the stage for merging helicopter and sonar technologies into an important operational capability. Accordingly, the Navy's first helicopter ASW squadron, HS-1, was commissioned at Naval Air Station Key West on October 3, 1951, and equipped with the lightweight tandem-rotor Piasecki HUP. This was followed by three more ASW helicopter squadrons commissioned in 1952. However, engine problems resulted in no HUP's being available for them to fly. The Marine Corps then helped out with a small number of HRS's, the utility equivalent of the HO4S.[57]

Meanwhile, in 1946, the Navy decided to become more deeply involved with helicopter experimentation and established Helicopter Development Squadron VX-3 at Floyd Bennett Field in New York on July 1. Under the direction of Commander Charles E. Houston, its mission was to evaluate fleet helicopter use, both ashore and afloat, initially with a complement of four HNS-1s and seven HOS-1s. In September 1946, VX-3 was moved to the Naval Air Station Lakehurst in New Jersey.

The rescue hoist was among the many innovations that VX-3 studied. In February 1947, a Sikorsky test pilot took a Sikorsky-owned, hoist-equipped S-51 aboard the aircraft carrier *Franklin D. Roosevelt* for a demonstration of this helicopter to the Navy. The hoist operator was Lieutenant Joseph Rullo of VX-3. In ten days they pulled six pilots and aircrewmen from the water around the *Franklin D. Roosevelt.*[58] The chief of naval operations quickly concluded that helicopters cut rescue time by approximately eighty percent.

Once the idea of fleet helicopter operations became accepted, development rapidly took place. On April 1, 1948 Helicopter Utility Squadron HU-1, the first of its type in the U.S. Navy, was commissioned at NAS Lakehurst under Commander M. A. Petters.[59] On January 27, 1949, the chief of naval operations authorized the conversion of all new-construction cruisers to accommodate helicopters.

On April 5, 1949 the decommissioning of the last of the observation squadrons, VO-2, marked the end of one era and the beginning of another as a plan to use helicopters in place of fixed-wing aircraft aboard battleships and cruisers was put into effect. The changeover was scheduled for completion by June 30 of that year.[60]

United States Marine Corps Developments

The United State Marine Corps specializes in amphibious warfare, and is capable of quickly placing seaborne troops ashore. Their finely tuned methods of amphibious assault landing operations, used most effectively during World War II on the beaches of Guam and Okinawa, were soon to be changed largely due to the efforts of Lieutenant General Roy S. Geiger, USMC.*

A man of vision, Lieutenant General Geiger wrote a letter in August 1946 to the commandant of the Marine Corps that laid the ground work that ultimately made helicopters a necessary part of Marine Corps amphibious warfare operations. In that letter, Lieutenant General Geiger stated:

> It is my opinion that future amphibious operations will be undertaken by much smaller expeditionary forces, which will be highly trained and lightly equipped, and transported by air or submarine, and movement accomplished with a greater degree of surprise and speed than has heretofore visualized.

Prompted by Geiger's letter, the Marine Corps began studying the helicopter's potential for ship-to-shore operations and formed Marine Helicopter Squadron (HMX-1) at Quantico, Virginia in December 1947. The squadron did not receive its first helicopters, two Sikorsky HO3S-1s, until February 9, 1948. This squadron would spend the next decades developing Marine Corps aviation tactics using a wide variety of helicopters.

---

*Lieutenant General Geiger led the Tenth Army to victory during the last days of World War II.

Although the Marine Corps soon realized the potential value of helicopters in amphibious warfare and quickly began investigating how best to use these machines, lack of funds and the limited range and load capacity of the early helicopters prevented much meaningful testing. However, despite these limitations, some progress was made.[61]

1947: The Year of Change for Army Aviation

The National Security Act of 1947 established the United States Air Force as an independent service. Two additional years of Army-Air Force negotiation was required to arrive at a basic agreement on the question of Army organic aviation.[62] The result severely limited Army aviation. Army fixed-wing aircraft were not to exceed 2500 pounds and rotary-wing craft were to weigh no more than 4000 pounds. Army aviation missions were restricted to observation of enemy forward areas, aerial route reconnaissance, control of march columns, camouflage inspections of ground force areas., local courier service, emergency wire laying, limited aerial photography and limited resupply. In 1951 another agreement eliminated the weight limitations and substituted a definition of functions. The missions allowed Army aviation were the same as those outlined in 1947. Another agreement, reached in 1952, placed a weight limit of 5000 pounds on Army fixed-wing aircraft.[63] This was the basis of the conflict between the two services during the Korean War.

The Malayan Emergency

British combat operations during the Malayan Emergency of the late 1940s and the early 1950s offer an interesting example of helicopter utilization in insurgent warfare. The British Army, fighting to save Malaya from communist insurgents, used rotary-wing aircraft on a large scale very effectively.

This war ran concurrently with the British support of the United Nations forces in Korea. The United Kingdom was one of the first countries to send troops to help the United States in South Korea. At the time, which was June 1950, they already had nearly forty thousand troops engaged in fighting Chinese communist guerrillas in Malaya. Because the Malayan Emergency began before Korea and preceded the United States' experience in Vietnam, it deserves examination in some depth.

The Vietnam War is often referred to as the ''helicopter war'' which implies that it was the first combat experience with substantial use of rotary-wing aircraft. The British Malayan experience reveals a story quite to the contrary. Although not of the same magnitude in terms of the number of aircraft and personnel involved, the Malayan Emergency spanned nearly twelve years beginning in 1948. It was the first true test of rotary-wing aircraft in anti-insurgent operations. And, unlike Vietnam, it was the only occasion in which communist aggression in Asia has been defeated.[1]

Beyond the Soviet Union's borders and its communist bloc countries, communism had been evident in varying degrees worldwide following World War II. Its influence was difficult to measure country by country for the period between 1945 and 1950. However, in Malaya and Southeast Asia, then known as Indo-China, the communists became organized and began utilizing guerrilla armies in the jungles of Malaya.

The communist movement existed in Malaya before the fall of Singapore during World War II. This movement was the basis of the Malayan Peoples' Anti-Japanese Army, which constituted the resistance movement throughout the Japanese occupation of Malaya.[2]

When the Japanese surrendered and came out of the Malayan jungles, they left behind large quantities of weapons and supplies. They also left as many as five thousand natives, of whom about twenty-five hundred were known to be communists. Their goal, to set up a communist state, was thwarted by the arrival of the British and the establishment of a British mission.[3] Fortunately, the British had gained some experience in jungle warfare during the Burma operations of World War II.

The British realized that the helicopter was a machine to be exploited in this jungle war because it was the only vehicle available that could safely perform counterinsurgency operations including troop transport, paratrooper drops, casualty evacuation, reconnaissance, communications and defoliation. These are all important elements when dealing with small bands of guerrillas.

Most of the Malayan peninsula is low-lying, except for some high ground which runs up through the western central side of the country. It is largely covered with primary jungle where the trees, with an average height of one hundred feet, obscure the ground from the air. There is little undergrowth in this type of jungle, and the ground surface is poor with little light. As a result, patrols could rarely be seen from the sky. The remainder of the country was covered by secondary jungle or cleared primary jungle which had been allowed to grow again. The undergrowth is very thick and there is a constant struggle for air and light. Rivers wind among the jungle and are often difficult to see until one is directly above them. Occasional clearings, which seemed to be good helicopter landing zones when seen from above, were often revealed to be waterlogged paddy fields upon closer inspection.

The weather is tropical. Winds are unpredictable at the heights at which helicopters operate, usually about two thousand feet. Violent turbulence can be experienced in the bowls at the ends of passes through high ground.[4]

Throughout the country the terrain favored the guerrillas. Air Vice-Marshal Sir Frances Mellersh described the country as particularly difficult for ground and air operations. The central spine of mountains, covered with dense jungle, reached a height of eight thousand feet. To the west of this ridge the country was fairly good, with a number of airfields including Alor Star, Port Swettenham, Penang and Singapore. But the east side was very poor, with practically no airfields.[5]

The terrain was such that there were few suitable helicopter landing sites. Finding landing zones required fixed-wing and helicopter teamwork. The usual procedure was for an Army Auster plane to locate a potential site first, and then guide a patrol to the appropriate clearing and give it instructions in the preparation of the landing area. The Auster then returned to the air strip where the helicopter was waiting and briefed the pilot. If necessary, the Auster would be used to guide the helicopter to the landing area.[6]

The guerrillas in Malaya enjoyed two significant advantages over the British Security Forces. In the first place, their flexibility was almost unlimited due to their ability to operate with very few supplies and their lack of concern with evacuating casualties—their sick and wounded were more often than not left to die in the jungle. Secondly, they always had the initiative in choosing where, when and how to attack. In a nutshell, the purpose of the combined air-supply and helicopter effort was to enhance the mobility and flexibility of the British forces to an extreme which largely neutralized the guerrillas' two biggest advantages.[7]

Although the Malayan Emergency was not an air war, aviation was essential to the success of the British Forces. Their role was to dominate the jungle fringes, thus separating the guerrillas from their supplies; to make jungle patrols and to help the civil administration resettle the Chinese squatters.[8]

Development of the land/air operations in Malaya fell into two phases. The first, from the beginning of the Emergency in June 1948, until the early part of 1953, was when the enemy was mainly on the jungle fringes. The second phase, from about March 1953 onwards, was when the guerrillas were forced to withdraw into the deep jungles by the increasing success of the British Forces.[9]

Helicopters were not the only aircraft used during this campaign. The air contribution was remarkably diverse, involving no fewer than eighteen different types of aircraft in some twenty subsidiary roles.[10] Fixed-wing air operations included reconnaissance, offensive air support and logistics operations. Helicopters were used primarily in logistics, medical evacuation and offensive air support crop spraying operations.

The advantages of the helicopter in its life saving role were considered to be speed in evacuation, flexibility of medical services, patient comfort, selective evacuation and economy. All of these reduced morbidity among casualties.[11]

Speed in medical casualty evacuation is most important in the cases involving the severely wounded. Casualties are a "perishable commodity," and therefore speed is paramount. Their speed over unfavorable terrain and their minimum landing site requirements favored the use of helicopters in forward fighting areas. This, in effect, placed hospitals and special treatment centers in direct support of the regimental or battalion surgeons.

Helicopter medevac also afforded the patient comfort, which is essential to preventing or minimizing shock. Vertical medevac also provided the range and flexibility needed to permit treatment at the facilities best equipped to handle the individual patient's particular injury.

During the Malayan crisis, calls for helicopter evacuation would occur on an average of about once a week. In addition to the task of rescuing Army casualties from jungle clearings, the helicopters were also useful for taking medical assistance to crashed aircraft and rescuing injured members of the crew. It was therefore recommended that each helicopter be outfitted with a winch with a sort of boatswain's chair attached to the end of the cable.[12]

First Request for Helicopter Evacuation

The first RAF Dragonflies arrived in Malaya in April 1950 and formed what was called the Casualty Evacuation (Casevac) Flight for rescue work over the jungle. On February 1, 1953, the Casevac Flight was expanded to form Squadron Number 194, the first helicopter squadron in the Royal Air Force.

The first call for helicopter medevac missions was made by Far East Headquarters in 1949, when Army patrols receiving casualties were unable to continue operations and had to hand-carry their wounded to the nearest road, a journey which often took several days. The helicopter called in to perform these missions was the Westland Dragonfly, which had never been operated in a tropical climate before.[13]

The Dragonfly could carry a crew of two and two passengers, cruise at 70 knots and, with full payload, had a range of 200 to 250 miles. Its cabin was not large enough to accommodate a patient on stretcher, so it was equipped with two special containers, or pods, mounted outside the cabin, one on each side of the aircraft. The pods were fitted with windows and controllable air vents, and had communication with the cabin.

Casevac Flight flew many missions of mercy over the next three years. A typical one took place in 1952 when a single Dragonfly, piloted by Flight Lieutenant J.R. Dowling, lifted a complete patrol of the Queen's own Cameroon, Highlanders from a small jungle clearing.[14]

Later, as helicopter usage increased, squadrons were organized under central control. The British Air Headquarters in Malaya eventually had three helicopter squadrons under its operational control: Number 194, equipped with Sycamores; Number 155, equipped with Whirlwinds of the Royal Air Force and Fleet Air Arm Squadron Number 848, equipped with American S-55s. All three squadrons were based at Kuala Lumpur Airfield, giving a total force of about twenty-six medium helicopters, used mostly for troop-lifting, and fourteen light helicopters, mainly used for casualty evacuation and communications.[15]

By 1952, the need for more helicopters in Malaya had become clear. Far East Command asked for twenty-four more, including six heavy-lift troop carriers, but Sir Gerald Templer, the newly appointed governor general, thought there should be fifty big troop carriers at least.[16] However, because manufacturing these flying machines was still a new art, the production rate of British-built helicopters was very slow. The British turned to the United States for help, but at the time the Mutual Defence Aid Pact with Britain contained reservations about providing assistance in a "colonial war," as the Malayan Emergency might have been termed.

The impasse was partially resolved by the diversion of a Royal Navy squadron equipped with American built S-55 Whirlwinds from the NATO antisubmarine force via a special arrangement with the President of the United States.[17] This squadron was Squadron Number 848, the Royal

Navy's first operational helicopter unit, formed at the end of October 1952. It made history as it arrived in the Far East on board the HMS *Perseus* in January 1953. Commanded by Lieutenant Commander Sydney Suthers, it sailed from Portsmouth on December 12, 1952, and on January 8, 1953, when near Changi Point, flew-off the aircraft to the Royal Naval Air Station at Sembawang on Singapore Island. Having conducted what is probably the first "flyoff," it became land-based in Malaya for operations over the jungle.[18]

With virtually no experience in jungle flight operations, Squadron 848's combat operations were approached with caution and a stern eye toward training. It appeared likely that their most exact flying would be into and out of jungle clearings, so it was decided to concentrate the training on work of this kind. First, a circle fifty feet in diameter was marked on the airfield, into which vertical descents from two hundred feet were made. Next, a similar area was cleared in some eighty-foot high rubber trees on the edge of the airfield and, lightly laden, the aircraft were taken into that. With familiarity came increased confidence, both in the helicopters and in themselves, and in a short time they were taking in maximum loads.

The squadron then turned to the final test: descents into two hundred-foot high primary jungle. There was none available for their use on Singapore Island, but the Army, which had a jungle training school in Johore, agreed to cut a clearing for them that they used daily.[19]

Training continued with indoctrination for those unfamiliar with helicopter operations. On January 21, three aircraft were detached to R.A.F. Kuala Lumpur for testing of aircraft performance, methods, equipment for the boarding and deplaning of troops, supply droppings, use of the external sling and the winching of casualties. Later, in conjunction with the R.A.F., methods of vegetation-spraying were employed.[20]

Toward the end of January 1953, Squadron 848 was given its first operational mission, a casualty evacuation, and from then on the work started to come in. On February 2, with the trials completed, Squadron 848 demonstrated its capabilities to representatives of the Army and the Police. Afterward, the missions increased dramatically. The aircraft performed well, and it soon became obvious that the squadron required additional pilots. Approval was readily given for them to be flown out from the United Kingdom.[21]

During its first year of operations in Malaya, Squadron Number 848 completed more than two hundred casualty evacuations. By the autumn of 1954, the total topped five hundred. The squadron was awarded the Boyd Trophy marking an "outstanding feat of naval aviation."[22]

Reconnaissance

During any military operation, knowing the enemy's movements is of vital importance, particularly when dealing with guerrillas. Therefore, reconnaissance missions were flown to obtain a constant flow of information on the location and movement of the terrorists, as well as other tactical and topographical information required by the security forces.[23] The helicopters were often used to attempt to pin-point the location of a terrorist camp, the whereabouts of which had been narrowed down to a mile or so, but which the fixed-wing patrol aircraft could not find.[24]

An interesting example of the use of helicopters for close-in reconnaissance was the successful location of some boats used by the terrorists along the shores of the Penerang Peninsula. For a long time, the terrorists crossed a particular river almost every night. They had to be using boats, but the location of the boats could not be discovered. Eventually a helicopter was put on the job, and after carefully examining each bank from a few feet up, the pilot spotted three boats completely submerged and cleverly concealed by mangrove trees.[25]

To obtain food supplies, the terrorists often planted small gardens in jungle clearings. From the air these were often easily located if they were along heavily traveled air routes. To assist in food denial, crop-spraying by aircraft was conducted, mostly using the Whirlwind helicopters of Squadron Number 155. A few Beavers and a Pioneer fixed-wing aircraft were also modified for use in this role.

The various missions were divided up among the available squadrons. Responsibility for coastal and river patrols, the protection of sea transportation and any coastal bombardment was assigned to the Royal Navy. The most important part played by the Air Force was airborne supply, without which jungle penetration would be limited by what a man could carry on his back. The transport squadrons in Malaya were continuously employed in maintaining essential services, including courier and ambulance flights ranging as far as Japan, Ceylon, Borneo, Australia and New Zealand. These aircraft were also employed in offensive ground support.[26]

Another interesting mission involved the use of fixed-wing support during helicopter operations in July 1952. A report was filed that told of a communist terrorist cultivation deep in the jungle, and that it seemed probable that there was a camp in the vicinity. The object of the operation was to locate the camp and destroy the crops. The plan called for troops to be lifted by helicopter to a position about four miles from the cultivation. From this position they would make a reconnaissance sortie and then attack the camp at dawn the following day. Intelligence indicated that there was a small natural clearing on the bend of a river at a suitable distance from the cultivation. However, they were unsure if the clearing was entirely suitable. It was decided to take three aircraft, two of which were fitted with winches, and to position them at the embarking point. The flight took off from Kuala Lumpur for the staging site where the aircraft were prepared for the following day's operations.

The next morning, at takeoff time, fog hovered over the camp. The

Hornet fighter escorts reported that the whole area was covered by low clouds. The Hornets had enough fuel to enable them to stay on their patrol line for a few hours. By 9:00 A.M. the clouds had lifted sufficiently for the helicopters to get airborne. Flying at two hundred feet above the jungle in a loose line astern they soon reached the clearing where they found that the landing site was definitely unsuitable for troop lift. Nearby, however, was a patch of secondary jungle with trees only seventy-five feet high. It was decided to drop the troops into that location. The S-55s hovered in turn over the selected spot and, one at a time, down through the trees the soldiers were lowered. At times they disappeared from the view of the winch operator. Fortunately, none got hung up. As soon as the first troops were in the clearing, the Hornets were dismissed. By the next sortie, the first clearing had been made large enough by the first troops for the helicopters to go in and hover at about eighteen feet. This allowed the troops to drop from the ends of the scrambling ropes. By 2:00 P.M. the mission was complete.[27]

About the time that Squadron Number 848 arrived in Malaya with their Whirlwinds, another helicopter was introduced into the conflict. Early in 1953, an example of the first British designed helicopters to see operational service, the Bristol Sycamore WA578, was delivered to the Far East and put through its paces in battle conditions.

In spite of some early apprehensions about the Sycamore's low-drooping rotor blades making it a dangerous aircraft to load and unload with casualties, it proved highly popular from the start with pilots who likened its handling characteristics to those of a sports car compared to the three-ton truck feel of a Dragonfly. There were other concerns too, mainly with the wooden blades in tropical conditions. But this aircraft, designed by the Austrian-born Raoul Hafner, went on to serve in the rescue role for another twenty years.[28]

Lessons Learned

One of the earliest lessons learned was that the stretcher pods mounted on the helicopters for transporting casualties interfered with the performance of the aircraft when operating in the tropics. They were eventually removed and a wickerwork "cradle," which was made locally, was attached to a metal rack fitted inside the cabin, with the foot end of the cradle projecting through the door. However, the patient was well protected by coverings.

It was not long before a new method was devised. It was known as the "top hat" modification and consisted of two large bulges in the fuselage to contain the head and foot of the cradle.[29]

The reliability, controllability and good maneuverability of the S-55 made it most suitable for operations in Malaya. Flying essentially an "off-the-shelf" aircraft, Squadron Number 848 found the S-55 reasonably well adapted to combat. For example, having the fuel tanks under the hold put the filler caps at a convenient level. This proved to be a great advantage, as fueling was invariably from 50-gallon drums via a 4-gallon tin and special chamois filter.

The squadrons found ways of dealing with the minor problems associated with the design of this aircraft. For example, one disadvantage was that there was only ten and one-half inches clearance under the rear fuselage. Without detriment to their anti-ground resonance properties, they increased the pressure in the main oleos, thus slightly increasing the ground clearance and at the same time lifting the tail rotor a trifle higher.[30]

The limited power of these early helicopters was a chronic problem and remained so in the Malayan tropical conditions. Finding a solution to this shortcoming was particularly challenging. The power of the engine in a helicopter is applied to the main rotor transmission and at the same time to the tail rotor drive shaft which is driven off the main transmission. In single rotor helicopters, the tail rotor is little more than an anti-torque device that keeps the aircraft pointed in the desired direction. On hot, humid days, often there was insufficient engine power available for a vertical takeoff. The helicopter pilots evolved a somewhat alarming procedure to give some final upward urge during a vertical takeoff in a jungle clearing. They knew that if they reduced the power delivered to the tail rotor by turning the whole aircraft in the same direction as the torque effect a bit more energy would be delivered to the main rotor and a few more precious feet around the tops of the trees might be obtained. The procedure called for the pilot to push on "right boot" at around tree-top height, not minding much which direction the aircraft finished up pointing in, but proceeding in that direction while thankfully obtaining some forward speed and much needed extra lift. Where one was and where one ought to go could be sorted out later.[31]

For the pilots, casualty evacuations were the most satisfying of all operations because here the helicopter was essential. Frequently a ten-minute helicopter lift saved a gravely injured man five days of being carried through the jungle—probably the difference between life and death.[32]

The question of cost versus capability surfaced during the Malayan conflict. Experience suggested that there were four main factors affecting the operations of helicopters. The first of these relates to operating costs. Discounting hoverheads, the direct cost of operating the two main types of helicopter in Malaya were:

Whirlwind medium helicopter______£78 per hour.
Sycamore light helicopter______£58 per hour.

The fixed wing aircraft used extensively were considerable less expensive to operate:

Pioneer aircraft______ £35 per hour.
Auster aircraft______ £13 per hour.

The high operating cost of the helicopters along with their capital costs made it necessary to exercise the utmost economy in their use. Where other means of transportation were available, helicopters were not used unless there were clear and overriding operational advantages to doing so. For example, during troop lifts as much of the journey as possible was done by rail, road or in fixed-wing aircraft in order to shorten the helicopter lift.[33] But often the use of helicopters was well worth the cost. Many times, ten minutes' flying saved a full day's march into the jungle, and enabled an operation to succeed where otherwise it might have failed.[34]

Perhaps the most important lesson learned was that helicopters are, by nature, multi-mission capable. The British learned that the same type of helicopter could be used in a variety of different roles. In Malaya, for example, the Whirlwind was used not only for troop-lifting, but also for casualty evacuation, reconnaissance, crop-spraying and paratrooping. Therefore, as in the case of fixed-wing aircraft, it was important that the control of helicopters was centralized at the highest practical level in order that their unique flexibility could be exploited to the fullest.[35]

Thus, the helicopter completed its first major test by fire in the jungles of Malaya. Its success was due both to the many capabilities of the machine itself and the courage and skills of the pilots who flew them. Korea was the next acid test and the results were just as impressive.

Top *The U.S. Navy's first helicopter was the Sikorsky HNS-1, obtained from the Army Air Corps.*

Bottom *Igor Sikorsky flying his newly-proven VS-300 helicopter in 1942 at Stratford, Connecticut. Al Krapish makes an in-flight tire change to demonstrate the stability of the aircraft.* Sikorsky Aircraft.

WN 342
DOBLHOFF

822

Opposite:
Top *A prototype helicopter, the Wn 342, was built for the German Navy for antisubmarine warfare in WWII. It never entered service.* Smithsonian Institute.
Center *The Focke-Achgelis Fa 61 was developed by Heinrich Focke in the 1930s and established several flight records.*
Bottom *The Piasecki HRP-1 Rescuer was an early heavy-lift helicopter. With a fabric cover and one Wright R-975 radial engine, its maximum gross takeoff weight was 6900 pounds.* Keystone.

Above *The Bell H-13, first flown on December 8, 1945, is the oldest helicopter still in service. Best known for its use in the* M.A.S.H. *movie and television series, it was used extensively in Korea for aerial observation and medical evacuation.* Bell Helicopter Textron.

BEWARE OF
TAIL ROTOR

Opposite:
Top *In 1948, the usefulness of helicopters in aerial spotting was demonstrated at the School of Artillery in Larkhill, England by the Royal Navy with the Sikorsky R-6 Hoverfly II.* Central Press Photos Ltd.
Bottom *Royal Navy Dragonfly (Sikorsky S-51) helicopters similar to this were used during the Malayan Emergency to locate enemy positions and to airlift casualties out of the jungle.*

Above *A U.S. Navy H-19, photographed in 1956.*
Below *In 1957, the USS* Mitscher *was the scene of tests to determine the feasibility of using helicopters to augment fleet antisubmarine warfare weapons systems. These tests eventually led to the development of the LAMPS program. The Bell HTL-7 shown here is equipped with two torpedoes.*

Opposite *Marines hold down a Sikorsky R-5 helicopter picking up casualties on a windswept slope in Korea.*

Top *A Vertol H-21C fires rockets during an Army exercise. It mounts .30-caliber and .50-caliber machine guns, twenty-four 2.75-inch rockets and has firing ports for eight M-1 rifles.*
Bottom *The Army's H-37, an early heavy-lift helicopter, was delivered in 1956. It was Sikorsky's first twin-engine helicopter; the main rotor had five blades, the tail rotor four.*

The Royal Navy's Whirlwind (Sikorsky S-55) helicopter was a significant improvement over the Dragonfly with increased power, maneuverability and cargo capacity.
Top *Whirlwind helicopters on the HMS* Bulwark *in 1960.*
Bottom *The Whirlwind in action during the Maylayan Emergency.*

Opposite *The Royal Navy continues to use the Wessex HU5 for commando support, troop transport and logistics. Introduced by Sikorsky in 1955, it has a single gas turbine engine mounted in the nose.* Ewart & Company, London.

ROYAL NAVY

Top *The Wasp is a single engine helicopter deployed aboard frigates and survey vessels of the Royal Navy. Its weapons include homing torpedoes, depth bombs and air-to-surface missiles. This Wasp is firing an SS11 missile.* HMS Osprey.

Bottom *Royal Navy Lynx helicopters can be configured with up to four lightweight Sea Skua antiship missiles.* Westland Helicopters Ltd.

Opposite *One of the most interesting concepts in rotorcraft design was the one-man lift system called the "Flying Donut" built by Hiller for the U.S. Army. The project was scrapped in 1960 because of control problems.* Hiller photograph.

Previous page *U.S. Marines of the 2nd Battalion, 7th Marine Regiment disembark from a CH-46 Sea Knight in Vietnam.*

Top *A U.S. Navy UH-1B Iroquois takes off from the USS* Harnett County *anchored in South Vietnam's Mekong Delta.*

Bottom *The U.S. Navy uses the Boeing CH-46 Sea Knight for combat support. A medium-lift cargo helicopter with a tandem rotor system, it can carry up to twenty-six troops.*

Opposite *The UH-1 Hueys of Helicopter Light Attack Squadron Three, the first and only active duty U.S. Navy attack helicopter squadron, were used as armed troop carriers and for close air support in Vietnam.*

Top *A UH-1B Huey with a door gunner during a search and destroy mission in Vietnam.*
Bottom *Two H-34 Choctaws pass over the city of Hue, near the demilitarized zone of Vietnam in 1966. Their machine guns could only be hard-mounted in the personnel door on the right-hand side.*

The Korean War

The "cold war" suddenly became hot on June 25, 1950 when the North Koreans poured over the border into South Korea on the pretext of repelling an invasion. With no declaration of war, the North Korean infantry crossed the thirty-eighth parallel in a full-scale invasion behind Russian-made tanks and marched toward Seoul.

Caught by surprise, and with their forces dispersed, the South Koreans offered little effective resistance. Two days later, the United Nations Security Council recommended that member states of the United Nations provide assistance to the Republic of Korea to repel the aggressors. That same day President Harry S. Truman authorized the use of air and naval forces to support South Korea, including a naval blockade of the Korean coast by the Seventh Fleet. On June 30, he ordered American ground forces into action.

It was a conflict that catapulted the world into modern warfare, with both sides exhibiting mobility, speed and flexibility of action. It was also a war that involved the use of two new and radically different types of aircraft: the jet and the helicopter. The first was a fast mover, capable of rapid aerial power projection, close air support and bombing missions. The second was a slow mover that made up for its lack of speed with maneuverability and multi-mission versatility.

The helicopter heretofore had not seen action in a conventional war, and its use in combat was still in the experimental stages. It would be a few years before the lessons learned by the British in Malaya would be widely known and appreciated. It would become increasingly clear that the helicopter could go places and do things in a way that conventional aircraft could not, and would make a measurable difference in the outcome of the conflict.

The Korean War provided the stage on which the helicopter's potential could once again be exploited in terms of its rescue, reconnaissance, liaison and transport capabilities. New concepts in the use of helicopters were developed such as command and control, mine spotting, vertical envelopment and combat logistics. These were relatively new roles for helicopters from the American perspective.

As for the enemy, these strange flying machines were generally perceived as no threat to their troops on the ground. However, during the

Korean War there was unofficial experimentation with gunship tactics and, for the first time, helicopters were a direct threat to enemy troops.

U.S. Marine Corps

Having had HMX-1 operational since 1947, the United States Marine Corps were leaders in the use of helicopters in combat. This is easily understood when one considers that during the Korean War helicopters were still so new that every tactic, every piece of equipment was innovative.[1]

In response to President Truman's orders, American ground forces were immediately committed to the fighting in Korea. Among them was the First Marine Brigade which included Marine Air Group (MAG) Thirty-Three. Under MAG-33 was the first Marine helicopter squadron to be trained for combat and sent to Korea, observation squadron VMO-6, based at Camp Pendleton, California.

Prior to this, VMO-6 was a fixed-wing squadron flying exclusively light OY-2 observation planes. It was augmented in July 1950 with four HO3S-1s,* seven officers and thirty enlisted men from HMX-1. Thus, it became the first composite squadron flying both fixed-wing and rotary-wing aircraft.

VMO-6 arrived at Pusan, South Korea, on August 2, 1950. While it routinely operated its eight OY-2s, the helicopter proved to be the source of most of its laurels.

The morning after arriving at Pusan, one of VMO-6's HO3S-1s was pressed into service with Brigadier General Edward A. Craig, USMC, aboard for a reconnaissance mission. This flight marked the dawn of a new era in command and liaison, because a general and his staff could now maintain direct contact with operations at the front such as had never been possible before.[2]

On August 4, VMO-6's HO3S-1s were again in action, this time to airlift Marine casualties out of the battle area near Chindong-mni. The HO3S-1s were not designed for medevac missions, and were hastily modified to carry one stretcher. The arrangement worked quite well, although the casualty's feet protruded through the cabin door in a manner similar to the way the British solved the problem in Malaya. Later, the helicopters were fitted with two external capsules just large enough to hold a stretcher case.

VMO-6's helicopters continued to support field operations with command, staff liaison, artillery spotting, rescue and casualty evacuation missions. Additionally, they often enhanced a fixed-wing strike mission by providing timely intelligence information on the target areas.

The seemingly fragile helicopter's vulnerability to enemy small arms fire had been in question, but after a short time in Korea these fears proved to be unfounded. One mission by the commanding officer of the Fifth Marines, Lieutenant Colonel Raymond L. Murray, was testimony

*The HO3S-1 was the equivalent of the British Dragonfly helicopter flown during the Malayan Emergency. The civilian designation was the Sikorsky S-51, which first flew in February 1946.

to the helicopter's survivability. While making a reconnaissance flight in the Chindong-mni area, his helicopter became the target of automatic and small arms fire at uncomfortably close range from North Korean troops hidden along both slopes of a narrow valley. But Pilot Gene Pope maneuvered the helicopter so skillfully, changing speed and altitude and taking every advantage of the terrain, that no harm resulted.[3]

Recognizing the value of vertical combat support and the need for greater lifting capacity, the first transport helicopter squadron in history, HMR-161, was formed by the Marines in 1951 at El Toro Air Base in California. Equipped with fifteen Sikorsky HRS-1s,* which could carry up to ten combat-equipped men, it was a major step forward in the evolution of the helicopter on the battlefield. This was a significant improvement to troop lift missions because, for the first time, a helicopter with sufficient lifting capacity was available for combat duty.

After several months of fighting and pushing the North Koreans back across the thirty-eighth parallel, on August 30, 1951, the helicopters of HMR-161 were placed under the command of the First Marine Division fighting in the rough mountain terrain of central Korea. These relatively new aircraft rapidly demonstrated their ability to carry troops and equipment into inaccessible areas of the battle zone. At one point they airlifted an entire battalion into position on top of a strategically important ridge when on September 20, 1951, twelve Marine Sikorsky H-19s lifted a company of 228 Marines and nine tons of supplies to a three thousand-foot hilltop in central Korea.

At the time, the shifting battle line was stabilized in the rugged mountainous terrain of central Korea. These were the first tests of the helicopter's ability to carry troops into inaccessible areas in a combat zone made by the Marine's First Division. Two experimental missions, Windmill I and Windmill II, were initiated with Sikorsky HRS-1 transport helicopters.

Windmill I, on September 13, 1951, was in an area of the Korean mountains extending from Inje to the Punch Bowl battle zone. It involved some twenty-eight flights in a period of a little more than fourteen hours. Nine tons of cargo were moved. On return trips, the helicopters evacuated seventy-five wounded men. Windmill II, in October 1951, was slightly less ambitious, involving just six tons of cargo hauled by ten helicopters.[4]

Tactical history was made by the First Division that fall which gave a glimpse of the future of warfare. But tactical development did not stop with the movement of troops. Another notable exercise used the H-19 for assault, battlefield transport and the evaluation of a new procedure known to the U.S. Marines as "hit an' git." This consisted of a system of flying a rocket launcher and its crew to a suitable firing position. They would land, fire a few rounds at the enemy position, then move on by helicopter, taking the still hot rocket launcher to a fresh firing position.[5]

*More popularly known as the H-19 Chickasaw, this helicopter was the same Westland-built Whirlwind that the British employed in Malaya. The civilian designation was the Sikorsky S-55 and it was first flown in November 1949.

These developments were the result of four years of research and testing by the U.S. Marines, who had used twelve of the U.S. Navy's small fleet of Piasecki HRP Rescuers to practice airborne assaults. Soon there evolved a new phrase, coined to describe the rapid movement and subsequent deployment of troops by helicopter: "vertical envelopment."[6] HMX-1 had begun experimenting with this concept at Quantico before the war.

U.S. Navy

World War II involved naval aviation in support of carrier fleet operations. In Korea, however, the mission of naval aviation was seldom direct support of the fleet or operations against enemy naval units. Carrier air patrol (CAP), antisubmarine and airborne early warning missions were performed, but most of the carriers' aircraft activity was devoted to operations against inland targets far beyond the range of the Seventh Fleet.[7]

Naval aviation did not take long to get into the Korean fight—eight days to be exact. The first carrier-based air attack against Pyongyang airfield was on July 3, 1950. From July to November 1950, naval air strikes were flown against other specific targets. In November 1950, naval aviation was assigned the mission of isolating the whole Korean battlefield south of the Tumen and Yalu Rivers. In the summer of 1951, naval aviation units were directed to implement "Operation Strangle." This involved the area between 38°15′ and 30°15′ north latitudes, a strip approximately fifty miles wide. The aviators were ordered to destroy all roads, bridges, railroad tracks and rolling stock. From December 28, 1951 to February 1, 1952 some 2782 cuts were made in railroad tracks, which almost completely halted eastern rail movements.[8]

A post-World War II innovation was the use of helicopters aboard the carriers as plane guards. This meant they provided airborne rescue services during carrier flight operations. Many Navy pilots owed their lives to the quick rescues affected by HU-1 detachment aviators.[9]

The first helicopters to see action in the Korean War were U.S. Navy HO3S-1s stationed aboard carriers. At the onset, the U.S. Navy used its helicopters primarily for rescue duties and general communications aboard aircraft carriers. Pilots for Helicopter Utility Squadron Two carried out extensive search and rescue operations, medical evacuation and mine spotting operations. But perhaps their greatest value was their positive effect on the morale of flight crews who knew they could be rescued by helicopter when performing strike and patrol missions behind enemy lines.

Early in the conflict, the North Koreans virtually ignored the helicopters as they made low passes during their various missions. The North Koreans' typical reaction was to simply hide behind trees or underbrush. Since the helicopters assigned to Korea were not configured with weapons, they were not seen as a threat. But the North Koreans' naive attitude did not last long.

Naval helicopters were the first to fire weapons in combat, although they did so unofficially. Lieutenant Junior Grade John W. Thornton, USN, and his crewman, Petty Officer Whitaker, performed some of the earliest helicopter light attack experiments when they fired .45-caliber pistols and carbine rifles at, and dropped hand grenades on, North Korean troops during their various missions over land. As early as January 1, 1951, Thornton and Whitaker began using their HO3S-1 as a "gunship." While their missions officially remained "search and rescue" and "mine and artillery spotting," they fired at the enemy when it became necessary. If they couldn't get fragmentation grenades from the ships they operated from, they would obtain percussion grenades, which were by themselves relatively harmless, and tape nails around them. That way, Thornton said, they could "nail them to a tree." These exploits were not well received by their fellow pilots because the North Koreans quickly learned that the helicopter was not merely a passive airborne vehicle. Unfortunately, these episodes went undocumented.

The North Koreans began to realize that the helicopter was a potential threat. Not only did they start to use small arms against them from the ground, but they also used airborne fire against them. In one reported incident, three Russian-type MIG-15 jets attacked a Navy HO3S-1 flown by Lieutenant Junior Grade Raymond A. Miller, USN, and his crewman Aviation Metalsmith Third Class R.F. Anderson, USN. This happened while they were rescuing twenty-eight South Korean troops from Changyon, deep in enemy territory. The helicopter had just left the ground with two South Korean soldiers aboard when it was attacked by the Russian jets. Only quick maneuvering by Lieutenant Miller avoided their being caught in the path of the enemy fire. Miller recounted later that the speed of the jets made it impossible for them to change their position to fire on the helicopter after it had maneuvered out of range. Before the jets had time to make a turn and come in for a second run the helicopter had flown out of sight and returned to its base ship.[10]

U.S. Air Force

The origin of helicopter evacuation in Korea was not the result of any preconceived plan; it was more or less just adopted for expediency. On August 3, 1950, the Army and the Air Force collaborated to test the concept of helicopter evacuation in the yard of a small college in Taegu, South Korea. As a result, the Army accepted helicopters for aeromedical evacuation and developed the first procedures for their use.

In November 1950, the Second Helicopter Detachment to be used for medical evacuation arrived in Korea. Initially assigned to the Seventy-Fourth Light Aviation Maintenance Company at Taegu, the unit spent the remainder of the year assembling their newly arrived Bell H-13s* to carry patients externally. On January 1, 1951, the Second Helicopter Detachment became operational and flew from Taegu to Seoul, where it was attached to the 8055th Army Unit.[11]

Helicopter operations were so successful that General Partridge, the commander-in-chief of the Fifth Air Force, directed the Third Air Rescue Squadron to station six of its nine H-5s (the USAF designation for the Sikorsky S-51) in Korea. At the same time, General Stratemyer, the Far East Air Force (FEAF) commander, asked the USAF to allocate twenty-five additional H-5s to form a special medical evacuation unit. Within a few days, fourteen H-5s from other commands were on their way to Korea.

By the end of August 1950 the Third Rescue Squadron's helicopters had flown eighty-three critically-wounded soldiers from the battle area. By then the helicopter unit had been designated "Detachment F." Under the command of Captain Oscar N. Tibbetts, USAF, they moved forward in the wake of the United Nations forces attacking northward from the Pusan perimeter.[12]

Rescue was the unit's mission and it went at it with a vengeance. On September 4, 1950, the USAF Thirty-Fifth Fighter-Bomber Squadron was hit by anti-aircraft fire. One pilot, Captain Robert E. Wayne, bailed out and landed safely. Half an hour later, a flight of F-80s flew combat air patrol overhead to ward off any marauding North Korean fighters while Captain Wayne was on his way out of enemy territory aboard a Sikorsky H-5 rescue helicopter. The machine was flown by Lieutenant Paul W. Van Boven, of the Far East Air Force's Third Rescue Squadron, who made history by becoming the first helicopter pilot to safely pluck a downed flyer from behind enemy lines.[13]

On March 23, 1951, two experimental Sikorsky YH-19 helicopters arrived in Korea to be evaluated under combat conditions. Twenty-four hours later they were working with the H-5s to evacuate wounded American paratroopers from the Munsan-ni area, just south of the thirty-eighth parallel, where the second largest paradrop of the Korean War had taken the Chinese completely by surprise. After two days of daylight operations, the H-5s and YH-19s had made a total of seventy-seven sorties into the Munsan-ni sector and evacuated 148 paratroopers. Operations continued until March 29, when the United Nations forces linked up with the paratroopers. By that time the number of helicopter sorties into the battle area had risen to 147.[14]

In June 1951, Detachment F was redesignated Detachment One, Third Air Rescue Squadron, and split up into four separate flights: one serving the 8055th Mobile Army Surgical Hospital, another attached to the U.S. Forty-Fifth Division command post near the center of the United Nations battle line, a third earmarked for use by the truce negotiators at

*The Bell H-13 Sioux, a two-place single-rotor light observation helicopter, was adapted for medevac missions by installing two stretchers on the sides of the pilot's bubble enclosure. This helicopter is best known for its regular appearances on the popular and long-running *M.A.S.H.* television series. The H-47 civilian version, first flown in December 1945, is still in use today in many countries after more than forty years of service.

Munsan-ni and the fourth on permanent alert at Seoul, now the detachment's headquarters.

By late January 1952, the H-5s that remained of Detachment One were worn out. Early the following month replacements arrived in the form of more capable Sikorsky H-19s.[15]

The H-19s were soon to prove their value. In July 1952, floods swept over part of the United Nations' battle line in Korea. When several forward elements of the United Nations' forces were trapped on high ground by the rising water, the helicopters lifted 710 soldiers out of danger.

Early in 1953 the air rescue detachments were reorganized. The detachments became squadrons, and the squadrons to which they belonged became groups. For example, Detachment One of the Third Air Rescue Squadron became the 215th Air Rescue Squadron of the Third Air Rescue Group. This procedure was adopted throughout the U.S. Air Force after March 1953.[16]

U.S. Army

The National Security Act of 1947, which established the United States Air Force as an independent service, made the Army responsible for aeromedical evacuation within the combat zone including battlefield pickup of casualties (except those from an airborne objective area supported by the Air Force), air transportation to initial point of treatment and any subsequent moves to hospital facilities within the Army combat zone. The National Security Act also limited Army aviation to two types of aircraft: fixed-wing not exceeding 2500 pounds in weight and rotary-wing, weighing not more than 4000 pounds. At the beginning of the war in Korea, the U.S. Air Force had most of the helicopters. The Army had only fifty-seven utility helicopters, Bell OH-13s.[17] Most of the equipment was obsolete, and the Army was forced to purchase "off the shelf" whatever aircraft came closest to meeting its requirements. The total number of Army aircraft would increase five-fold by mid-1954 as a result of the war.

As the Army had been investigating the use of helicopters for several years, it already had a good feel for their capabilities. It became increasingly impressed with the helicopter during the Korean War, and immediately wanted more helicopters for front line medevac services. The weight restrictions and the combat zone operational limitations soon caused bickering between the Air Force and the Army. The differences were partially resolved with an agreement stipulating that which helicopters the Army could own would be determined solely by function and not by weight. Thus, air transportation of Army supplies, equipment, personnel and small units within a combat zone of fifty to one hundred miles became a primary rather than a limited or emergency Army function.

The Korean War convinced the Army that having both fixed- and rotary-wing aviation under its control was indispensable. Generals Douglas MacArthur and Matthew Ridgeway both pressured the Department of the Army to approve more funds and equipment for aviation and to dispatch more helicopters to Korea. However, few of these additional helicopters reached the Far East in time to serve in the conflict.[18]

With Army aviation's involvement in the Korean War, the World War II concept of direct aviation support for the ground commander was further developed. New aircraft such as the L-19 Bird Dog, the H-13 Sioux and the H-19 Chickasaw helicopters were introduced and used extensively for reconnaissance and artillery spotting. These aircraft further expanded the limits of airmobility and aeromedical evacuation of casualties.[19]

The first Army helicopters did not arrive in Korea until late in December 1950. They were Bell H-13s, two-seat helicopters destined for the liaison and artillery spotting roles, but which also had a limited casualty evacuation capability. Four H-13s were assigned to the Second Army Helicopter Detachment at Seoul and began operations in January 1951 with Captain Albert Seburn, USA, as the commanding officer. By the end of the month, the detachment had evacuated more than five hundred casualties from the battle area. The four helicopter pilots involved were each awarded the Distinguished Flying Cross.[20]

In January 1951, the H-13s were augmented with a small number of two-seat Hiller H-23 Ravens which had been sent to Korea for combat evaluation. During 1951 both types were used increasingly for combat surveillance. It was not until May 1953 that the first Army cargo helicopter unit, the Sixth Transportation Company equipped with twelve Sikorsky H-19C's, arrived in Korea. That month, during a three-day exercise called "Skyhook," these helicopters were used to supply three front-line infantry regiments. In June, joined by the Fifteenth Helicopter Transportation Company, the Sixth put the experience it had acquired to good use when it airlifted supplies to an infantry regiment cut off from ground support, enabling it to hold its position in the face of determined communist attacks.[21]

Credit for the first Army helicopter evacuation in Korea is shared by First Lieutenants Willis G. Strawn and Joseph L. Bowler, USA. On January 3, 1951, Lieutenants Strawn and Bowler flew their H-13s from Seoul to an area about sixty miles northeast of Seoul. Each picked up one wounded American soldier and returned to an Army hospital in Seoul. Late in 1951, Lieutenant Bowler established a Korean War medical evacuation record. In ten months he had accomplished 821 medical evacuations in 483 sorties. Both Strawn and Bowler were awarded the Distinguished Flying Cross for their efforts in Korea.[22]

In January 1951, the Third and Fourth Helicopter Detachments arrived in Korea with minimum operating personnel and four H-13 aircraft each. The following February, the First Helicopter Detachment arrived. At the time, all helicopter detachments used for medical evacuation were assigned to the 3035th Army Unit, Eighth Army Flight Detachment. The early days of these helicopter evacuation detachments were quite stormy, reflecting the chaos of Korea itself in early 1951. The Fourth Helicopter Detachment suffered a complete breakdown of all its aircraft and was returned to the rear for reequipping. It did not become operational until March 1951. The First Helicopter Detachment never became operational, and was ordered non-operational on May 14, 1951.

The three operational detachments performed exceptionally well despite recurrent maintenance problems, especially shortages of high octane gas and spare parts. With only eleven reconnaissance helicopters, they evacuated 1935 patients during the first six months of 1951. This record is even more remarkable when it is realized that only one or two patients could be evacuated per sortie.[23]

Not until l950 did the Army and the Bell Company collaborate on experimentally arming the OH-13 helicopter. The first official use of the armed helicopter in combat can be attributed to the U.S. Army in Korea: an OH-13 with a bazooka. However, the French in Indochina also take credit for allegedly flying OH-13s configured with machine guns.

The Sixth Transportation Company with H-19s arrived in Korea in December 1952 and became the first Army transportation helicopter company to support units engaged in combat.[24]

During the first half of 1951, crucial battles of the war were fought as the Chinese attempted to overwhelm the United Nations' Army. Increasingly, helicopters were used by battlefield commanders for close surveillance of the battle situation and for landing right in the combat area. In these roles, they were plainly superior to fixed-wing aircraft.[25]

Army aviation entered a period of rapid expansion and change after 1952. The advantages of transporting troops by helicopter into combat became apparent to the United States. As early as July 1952, Secretary of the Army Frank Pace, Jr. recognized the far-reaching and revolutionary concepts inherent in the applications of the machine to the battlefield, and promoted the research and development of new models and new applications. One of his most important contributions was to encourage the aircraft industry to improve the state of the art helicopter.[26]

In August 1952, the Department of the Army authorized the Helicopter Ambulance Unit, TOE 8-500R, Cell RA. This detachment contained five reconnaissance helicopters, seven Medical Service Corps pilots and essential supporting personnel and equipment. In December 1952, the operating detachments in Korea were reorganized under TOE 8-500R. Designated medical detachments, helicopter ambulance, they became medical units for first time. In the spring of 1953, two additional helicopter ambulance detachments were organized in Korea—one operational and the second a "paper" organization.[27]

Army interests and activities in aeromedical evacuation were not limited to the Korean battlefields nor did they cease with the end of that war. In November 1952, an Army Aviation Section was established in the Medical Plans and Operations Division of the Office of the Surgeon General. This was set up to monitor and supervise aviation medicine and aeromedical evacuation activities within the Office of the Surgeon General.[28]

In late 1952, the Brooke Army Medical Center at Fort Sam Houston, Texas, was selected as the site for activation, training and deployment of medical helicopter ambulance detachments. On October 15, 1952, the Fifty-Third Medical Detachment, Helicopter Ambulance Unit, was organized. The redesignation of operating detachments in Korea followed by about two months. Within one year, five helicopter ambulance units had been activated at this center.[29]

More Lessons Learned

A review of the helicopters' role in the Korean War must include two important points: maintenance and new applications.

The helicopter was a relatively new machine to be exploited in this short but tough war, and it was in great demand for medevac services. It became so essential in this mission that maintenance developed into a serious problem. The field facilities for repair and servicing were, for the most part, inadequate. Sometimes the use of the equipment was so vital that mechanics found no rest or relief from the bitter cold. Virtually every component wanted helicopters: supply commands, communications squadrons, personnel and so on up the line. Naturally, this added to the burden on the supply side.[30]

The Air Force used H-5s and H-19s to evacuate the wounded and rescue downed pilots. The Marine Corps used their H-19s to resupply isolated outposts, and took the first steps to developing what they called "vertical envelopment" tactics. The Bell H-13 made a name for itself by rushing battlefield wounded directly to the various U.S. Army M.A.S.H. units behind the front. Korea demonstrated that the helicopter was up to the rigors of war. Soon, the helicopter would become one of the most important players in the war over the horizon . . . the war that became known as "The Helicopter War."

Between January 1, 1951, and the cessation of active hostilities on July 27, 1953, helicopter detachments under the control of the Army Medical Service evacuated a total of 21,212 casualties. The availability of forward helicopter evacuation contributed considerably to achieving what was then the lowest mortality rate of wounded reaching medical channels of any major war. [31]

All this is testimony to the importance of this new equipment to the soldier in the field. The helicopter came of age virtually overnight.

Even after the fighting stopped, helicopters continued to carry out important missions. Army aviators played prominent roles in "Operation Little Switch," which involved the exchange of wounded or sick prisoners of war from April 20 to April 26, 1953. Helicopter pilots of the Fiftieth Medical Detachment evacuated the United Nations' prisoners from the exchange site at Panmunjom to field hospitals near Munsan-ni (dubbed Freedom Village). The wounded were then taken from Munsan-ni to other rear areas by the H-19s of the Sixth Transportation Company.[32] Captain Gaddis, commanding officer of the Fiftieth Medical Detachment, evacuated the first two wounded: a Turkish soldier and an American.

During the Korean War it was decided that while there was a need for direct medical control of ambulance aircraft, there was no requirement for special purpose ambulance aircraft from the design or procurement standpoint. Instead, the policy was adopted that whenever practical all Army aircraft would be designed for transporting patients as an ancillary function.[33] From that point on, virtually every U.S. military helicopter was to have a secondary mission of medevac.

A comparison of the medical load capabilities of helicopters during the late 1950s and early 1960s shows the progress that was to be made after Korea:

AIRCRAFT	TYPE	CONFIGURATION
Korean War		
OH-13	2 litters	external
OH-23	2 litters	external
UH-19	6 litters	internal
Post-Korean War		
UH-1A	2 litters	internal
	1 ambulatory	
UH-1D	6 litters	internal
CH-21	12 litters	internal
CH-34	8 litters	internal
CH-37	24 litters	internal
CH-47A	24 litters	internal

On June 23, 1951 the Soviets proposed that cease-fire discussions be undertaken. On July 10 the discussions began at Kaesong, but were soon interrupted, and then moved to Panmunjom on October 25. For nearly two years the negotiations continued with frequent suspensions and, at times, bitter arguments.

A truce was finally agreed upon, and the fighting ceased on July 27, 1953, Korean time. On the last day of hostilities, virtually until the truce was officially signed, the U.S. Navy's four attack carriers, with twenty-one squadrons among them, were still hammering away at the enemy. And the helicopters were there.

Post-Korean War Developments

Following the Korean War, rotary-wing development took a turn for the better. Unlike the post-World War II demobilization's adverse affect on helicopter design and military use, this period was quite different. The imaginations of the engineers were fired by the dramatic exploits and successes of the helicopters in the Korean conflict and fueled by technological breakthroughs. The goal was simple: to develop larger helicopters suitable for combat operations that were more capable, more reliable and easier to maintain. Attention was given to defining missions more carefully and to developing helicopters to satisfy them.

As of July 1, 1954, U.S. Army aircraft numbered 3615 on hand and an additional 1040 on order. They were divided into seven categories: observation, utility, command and cargo fixed-wing aircraft; and reconnaissance, utility and cargo helicopters.

The Sky Cavalry

Immediately after the Korean War, the Army began to methodically exploit the helicopter's combat uses. The individual who spearheaded this initiative was General Matthew B. Ridgeway, USA, a man of great courage, leadership and vision.

In December 1950, then Lieutenant General Ridgeway took command of the Eighth Army in Korea following the death of General Walton H. Walker. In January 1952, he skillfully commanded the Eighth Army during one of the strongest communist offensives of the war. After being forced to withdraw, he lead a counteroffensive on January 24 and by April 23 the communists were driven back across the thirty-eighth parallel. It is safe to say that General Ridgeway witnessed the helicopter's true value on the battlefield.

General Ridgeway, as Army chief of staff in January 1955, reorganized aviation in the Army and by so doing provided a sound foundation for the development of what became known as the "sky cavalry" (or "sky cav") concept. He chose as his first Director of Army Aviation Major General Hamilton Howze, one of the leading supporters of this concept. General Ridgeway's reorganization included the establishment of the U.S. Army Aviation Center at Fort Rucker, Alabama, which also housed the U.S. Army Aviation School. Under General Howze's leadership, the "sky cav" concept took root.

Another strong advocate of the helicopter was Major General James M. Gavin, who in 1954 pointed out that the cavalry started out on the back of an animal and later switched to armored vehicles, and if Lieutenant General Walton H. Walkers' Eighth Army cavalry in Korea could have been switched to helicopters, the Chinese may not have been able to strike with such complete and overwhelming surprise in 1950. General Gavin's theories led to General Howze's support of the "sky cav" idea, which was a reconnaissance unit mounted in helicopters. The concept was tested under many names, but all had the same objective: to extend the eyes and ears of the commander farther and faster to do a better job.[34]

A New Helicopter

While the tactical concepts were being reshaped by the Army brass, the hardware was also going through the early phases of evolution. In January 1955, a design competition was held to select the new standard Army utility helicopter. Great emphasis was placed on the aeromedical evacuation function. The winning design was Bell's HU-1A Iroquois, later designated UH-1 when helicopter designations were standardized in 1962. It was frequently referred to as a "helicopter ambulance," in spite of the fact that it was a general purpose utility helicopter with a variety of functions.[35] The HU-1A was a two-bladed single rotor helicopter with one 700 shaft horse power (SHP) T53-L-1A turboshaft engine. It was delivered to the Army in June 1959. It was so successful that Bell ultimately produced more than nine thousand in various configurations, many of which are still flying today.

In tactical theory, however, progress was slow because the concepts had to be thoroughly explored before a course of action could be developed. "Operation Sagebrush," a joint Army/Air Force exercise in 1955 tested many concepts, including aerial cavalry and limited infantry transport.[36] This exercise was important because it dramatized the Army's acute need for much greater mobility on the modern battlefield.

In 1955, the "helicopter gunship" concept surfaced and in 1956 the U.S. Army began fabricating and testing helicopter armament at Fort Rucker, Alabama. This was a special project of Brigadier General Cal I. Hutton, USA. The major consideration for this project was the need to provide suppressive fire for assault troops.[37] This need became apparent when the H-19s were deployed in Korea because of their vulnerability during troop assault landings. Earlier efforts had included mounting a bazooka on an H-13 helicopter in 1950 and a makeshift grenade launcher, also on an H-13, in 1953.

The main problem encountered was weapon inaccuracy, caused by the helicopter's inherent instability.[38] Many experiments were conducted by the Fort Rucker group and in March 1957, the Aviation Center directed the organization of a provisional Sky Cavalry Platoon. This test unit was reorganized by the Third Army General Order in March 1958, and redesignated as the 7292nd Aerial Combat Reconnaissance (ACR) Company (Experimental). The 'Sky Cav' crew worked hard developing weapons systems for Army helicopters and experimenting with machine guns (.30- to .50-caliber), rockets (up to five inch) and various cannons.[39] These studies ultimately led to further experimentation and establishment of an aerial combat reconnaissance company in 1958.

U.S. Marine Corps Developments

Between the end of the Korean War and its involvement in Vietnam, the U.S. Marine Corps continued to pursue larger and more capable helicopters. Based on the Korean War experience, the Marines were concentrating on the "vertical" element of amphibious assault operations. Their immediate concern was moving men and equipment ashore quickly and reliably.

The Sikorsky HR2S single-rotor, twin reciprocating-engine helicopter was obtained in 1956 because of its enormous lifting capacity. Able to carry five thousand pounds of cargo or twenty combat ready Marines, this enormous flying machine reigned as the largest lifting helicopter until the CH-53A was introduced some ten years later.

Antisubmarine Warfare

Between 1946 and 1951, helicopters in the U.S. Navy had become well established in utility and search and rescue missions. However, the early concept of using them for antisubmarine warfare had not been fully explored. The 1950s marked the beginning of the maturity of the naval helicopter largely because of new testing techniques and the availability of new technology.

The Navy's VX-1 at Key West, Florida, had been tasked with rotary-wing ASW experimentation. With the development of the new variable depth "dipping" sonar by the Bureau of Aeronautics and the Naval Air Development Center in Johnsville, Pennsylvania, VX-1 commenced testing the Piasecki HRP helicopter. The trials were successful enough to eventually incorporate helicopters into fleet ASW operations.

The advantages of using rotary-wing aircraft with the underwater sensor became evident as a great deal of study was conducted to determine its benefits. The dipping sonar device was installed inside the helicopter's cabin on a large reel. This allowed the helicopter to hover close to the water in a fixed location and lower the sonar sensor to the best depth for submarine searches. It was learned that the dipped sonar transducer lies motionless in the water and is not affected by the rush of water produced by a destroyer moving rapidly nearby. Also, it was discovered that lowering the sonar at selected depths could reduce the adverse effects of water temperature gradients and salinity. Furthermore, the dipped sonar can be transported at will, and at greater speeds than the destroyer sonar of the target. Most importantly, the helicopter was invulnerable to submarine surface attack and so did not need to exercise caution in its approach to a known target.[40] Once the target was acquired, the helicopter could drop either conventional depth bombs or homing torpedoes.

News from the fleet began coming in regularly as to the effectiveness of helicopter participation in antisubmarine exercises. For example, in a report of 1953 Hunter-Killer exercises, the commander of Carrier Division Seventeen succinctly described the helicopter's success: "twenty-one missions, twenty-one contacts."[41] He went on to say that helicopters seemed to have a great potential for reducing time lag to datum,*

*Datum was the term for a suspected submarine contact.

positively identifying the contact, tenacity in holding contact and the ability to regain contact with speed.

As successful as these experiments were, the helicopters used for ASW were designed and built as transports for the Army and the Marine Corps. Initially, a few HRS Marine helicopters were borrowed by the Navy in order to try them out in the ASW program. Most of the changes that had to be made were initiated by squadron personnel. In turn, these changes were incorporated into helicopters designed specifically for ASW work. The Navy ASW squadrons were using the Sikorsky H04S-3 (H-19) helicopter with a crew of two pilots and one sonar operator. Teams of two to fifteen helicopters operated from the decks of aircraft carriers or from special landing platforms on much smaller vessels.[42]

The helicopters earned their passage on the crowded carrier decks with the protection they provided from submarine threats. They were what we would call today "force multipliers": that is, they did much more than just one mission and in effect increased the submarines' tactical problems. No longer did the submarine commander have to deal only with a few destroyers or fast frigates around the aircraft carrier, but he also had to carefully consider the swarm of highly mobile "pingers." He could never be sure exactly where they were or when they would engage him.

The helicopters pursued the submarines with skill and courage. Even when the they failed to make a contact during certain phases of the operations, their presence in the area forced the submarines to change their tactics, even to lie dead in the water or to run away to avoid detection. When the submarine is held down or forced to leave the area, the task force or convoy is then free to proceed unmolested on its way.

On the flight decks of the carriers, the helicopters had to be fast. Experiments showed that seven helicopters could be launched in thirty-five seconds. If nine helicopters were being used, with two being brought from the hangar deck, only three minutes and thirty seconds were required.[43]

Once again, technology was having a dramatic impact on helicopter ASW development. In 1955, new high-powered helicopters with sonar gear specifically designed to do antisubmarine warfare were being developed. The Sikorsky twin turboshaft, single-rotor SH-3A Sea King was just a few years away. It was first delivered to the Navy in 1961 and was the first helicopter designed specifically for the ASW mission, although it served in many other roles as well. The SH-3 is still flying ASW missions in many of the Navy's squadrons and will soon be replaced in its carrier-based role by a variation of the Sikorsky SH-60F Seahawk helicopter.

Because of the poor state of the art of avionics in 1955 the helicopter was essentially a "fair weather bird." It could not successfully or safely perform its mission at night or under inclement conditions. It was very unstable in a hover and, when compared to fixed-wing aircraft, relatively unstable in forward flight.[44] But all that progressively became less problematic with the introduction of the SH-34 Choctaw in the late 1950s and the SH-3A in the early 1960s. The SH-3A was the first true all-weather ASW helicopter which, with its sophisticated stabilization systems, was able to perform day and night sub-hunting operations.

Summary

The post-Korean War period saw a renaissance of rotary-wing aircraft development. Helicopters had been experimented with in actual combat and, although they were off-the-shelf machines, they performed reasonably well. Their performance was at least sufficient to reveal the unique value of their capabilities in combat. New missions surfaced as quickly as the avionic, power plant and rotary-wing design technologies became available.

The French-Algerian War

Helicopters in Korea were used primarily for casualty evacuation, search and rescue, observation and troop transport. Other than the use of personal firearms by a few individuals, weapons were not used on board helicopters.

In the mid-1950s, the French were presented with an opportunity to exploit the helicopter's "gunship" potential in actual combat. This development was particularly timely because the helicopters available were able to handle the weapons employed. The lighter helicopters of the Korean war and earlier were not stressed to handle firearms.

Almost as soon as the French began pulling out of Southeast Asia during the fall of 1954, they became involved in yet another guerrilla war, this time in Algeria. On November 1, 1954, a Muslim guerrilla rebellion erupted with the goal of independence. They called themselves the Front de Liberation Nationale (FLN).

To put down the rebellion, France sent some 500,000 troops to Algeria. Their success was not to come for many reasons, and after nearly eight years of fighting, President de Gaulle proclaimed Algeria's independence from France on July 3, 1962.

Nevertheless, this guerrilla war presents an excellent opportunity to study one of the earliest experiments in integrating firepower with rotary-wing aircraft. It was an excellent proving ground for learning how the helicopter could be used in the assault role under adverse conditions. Throughout this conflict, helicopters were effectively used to improve the mobility and to reduce the response time of the French troops. The successes they realized encouraged the French to expand their helicopter fleet.

By the time the Algerian War ended, the French had over six hundred helicopters operating in transport, evacuation, reconnaissance and fire support roles. The last role was a new one, never before tested in actual combat.[1] Until the operations in North Africa started, the helicopter had been used primarily for logistics and support.

The helicopter gave the French Army greater flexibility for conducting operations, transporting troops and firepower to rebel fighting hot spots with speed and relative ease. This was because it greatly reduced one of their largest obstacles—terrain. The 750 mile Mediterranean coastal zone is mountainous and rocky. East of Algiers, the Great and Little Kabylia mountains rise as high as 7570 feet; the rest of the country is mostly high rough plateau and desert. The helicopter was the only vehicle capable of enhancing mobility under these conditions. In short, the helicopter promised to save the Army time and fatigue.[2]

The rebellion was not felt throughout the entire country. Only the northern portion strongly supported rebel activity, which flourished in the large coastal cities of Oran, Algiers and Constantine. Large numbers of French troops were assigned to deal with these urban terrorists.[3]

The French Army's helicopter operations consisted principally of transporting troops, individual arms, wounded and supplies. However, the French quickly determined that the armed H-34 troop transport and cargo helicopter could be utilized for an additional mission—as an airborne gun platform. They studied this application in detail and developed many innovative tactics.

In the first use of helicopters as troop assault vehicles, they were employed in small increments in conjunction with other air and ground units. This application was not developed before the conflict, but rather during the fighting. It came to be known as "airmobililty."

The term "airmobility" was used earlier by the French to describe the capability of a military unit to use air space to free itself from the limitations imposed by terrain. It was a generic term used in reference to all airborne missions and operations. The term eventually took on a more specific meaning to include not only the capability of air movement, but also airborne support of ground troop operations.[4]

The French Army distinguished two forms of airmobile operations. The first allowed a unit to move easily by helicopter. An artillery battery moved by helicopter is an "airmobile battery." The second provided more of the basic elements of military operations such as reconnaissance, fire and transportation. Heliborne command and control and armed helicopters are also part of the airmobility concept. By either definition, airmobility was designed and used to support ground troop operations. Because of the limited helicopter assets available, airmobility was employed according to the priorities set by the troop commander.[5]

The French discovered that the rebel guerrillas in Algeria enjoyed many of the same advantages as the terrorists in the Malayan jungles. They were native to the country where the fighting was taking place and perfectly adapted to it. They enjoyed the support, more or less, of the general population. They spoke the languages, practiced the religion and knew the local habits. They could lose themselves among the population and emerge at the time of their choosing.[6]

Airmobility helped the French reduce the effectiveness of many of these advantages. They highly regarded the value of armed helicopters in fighting guerrillas.

Armed Helicopters

The French first officially operated armed helicopters in combat during a battle with Muslim rebel forces in the heart of the Aures, a group of peaks in the Atala Mountains. During this incident, a clever French unit commander decided to arm a helicopter and strike rebel positions. The French unit was pinned down by rebel fire from a hillside above their position. The ground troops could not get into a position where they could provide a base of fire. The commander had an observation helicopter with two litters attached to its sides. He strapped a man with an automatic rifle in each litter and sent the helicopter up against the rebels, who were routed from their position by the helicopter's fire. Thus, the French unit was able to occupy its objective.[7]

This rather primitive, but successful, beginning led to more sophisticated hardware and tactics. The helicopters employed during the Algerian uprising were the Sikorsky S-55 (H-19) and the S-58 (H-34), the Vertol H-21 (for troop transports and logistics), the Bell H-47 (H-13) and the Sud-Est Alouette II, a French turbine powered helicopter of about the same size as the Bell 47 but with greater lift capability and power (used for medical evacuation, reconnaissance and liaison).

The French Army aviation units consisted of light aircraft platoons (VMO), one to a zone, and one helicopter group—Army Helicopter Group Number Two—based at Setif in the Constantine area. Its helicopters were the same as those of the Air Force Groups, except that it used the H-21 as its primary troop assault helicopter. The light helicopter squadrons of both services had been assigned, in units of one or two, to the widely dispersed garrisons and placed under their operational control. As they were utilized primarily for evacuation purposes, such decentralization was essential for the swift removal of the wounded to base hospitals.[8]

The main command utilizing planes and helicopters organic to the French Army in Algeria was known as Groupement ALAT 101, located in eastern Algeria at Setif. The second unit, similar to ALAT 101, was known as EA/ALAT. It was located in western Algeria at Sidi-bel-Abbès. Its mission was to train operational pilots and it did not engage in combat. It had approximately ten H-21s, ten H-19s and thirty assorted fixed-wing aircraft.[9]

The missions and the areas of operation in Algeria were shared between the French Army and Air Force. The Army operated its helicopters in eastern Algeria, while the Air Force operated in western Algeria. This arrangement began with the introduction of the H-21 and H-34 helicopters to Algeria in June 1956.

The Groupement ALAT 101 was divided into two helicopter detachments of seven H-21s and one Alouette each, referred to as basic combat "cells." When a cell was placed in combat, typically six H-21s and two

Alouettes were used. The spare H-21 was held in standby in case one was lost in combat. The second Alouette was provided by the Alouette Squadron.

In October 1959, during some of the hottest fighting in the Atlas Mountains and along the Tunisian border, four Helicopter Intervention Detachments (DIH's)* at Setif provided support. Helicopter Intervention Detachments stationed at Guelma and Tibessa also supported the fighting along the border.

These helicopter detachments were designed to be mobilized within an hour and to be self-supporting. That is, they did not require fixed installations.

Helicopter Armament, Tactics and Armor

Because the helicopters were drawn into close combat, they were subjected to a great deal of small arms fire. Accordingly, survivability became an increasingly important matter as the fighting continued. Both weapons and armor were used to deal with the problem: the weapons suppressed the ground fire while the armor offered protection to the flight crews as well as the aircraft.

The French Air Force's policy was to arm one in six helicopters. These helicopters did not carry troops. Their sole job was to provide very close-in air support immediately prior to and during an assault landing. A flexible, mounted rapid-fire weapon at least one caliber greater than the ground based weapons was used. The helicopters orbited over the drop zone and directed fire where it was needed most.[10]

The H-21 armament system initially used by the French was based on the prototype installation developed jointly by the U.S. Army Combat Development Group at Fort Rucker, Alabama and Boeing-Vertol in early 1957. The pilot could fire the 68 mm SNEB rockets and .30-caliber machine guns mounted on each side of the helicopter by using the "grip hoist switch" and the "spare micro-switch" buttons respectively. The thirty-six 68 mm rockets mounted on the frame were eventually replaced by seventy-two 37 mm Type 412 SNEB rocket pods. The wider dispersal of fire was preferred for dealing with guerrilla targets.[11]

The French Army considered one of the best armament suits for the H-21 helicopter to be two .30-caliber machine guns with 250 rounds each (with one round in five using incendiary tracers) and seventy-two 37 mm SNEB rockets. For the Alouette II they preferred to use the seventy-two 37 mm SNEB rockets exclusively.[12]

The naval H-21s were each equipped with a swivel mount in the doorway for a 20 mm cannon. There were several types in use: the World War II German MG151 (rated at seven hundred rounds per minute), the M-3 and the English HS-404 (each rated at six hundred rounds per minute). The HS-404 was considered the most satisfactory.

In troop assault operations, immediately before the landing of the

*Detachment d'Intervention d'Helicoptere

troop-carrying helicopters the landing zone was well-saturated with gun fire. The French believed that the fact that they had lost no helicopters due to enemy ground fire since adopting this tactic was sufficient to justify its continued use.[13] During these landing operations, the Army preferred a straight-in fast pass over the Air Force's orbiting method. The orbiting helicopters were unnecessarily exposed to ground fire and more easily shot down.

During this period, the French were also spearheading the development of antitank missile systems. The SS-10 ground-to-ground antitank missile of the early 1950s was followed with a larger, longer-ranged version called the SS-11 in 1956. An air-launched version, the AS-11, was tested on the Alouette II in 1958.[14] It was believed that there was a significant advantage to the aerial delivery of antitank missiles in the larger silhouette presented by the target from the air. Helicopters could therefore engage tanks from a variety of angles. Thus helicopters provided a new dimension to armed combat.[15] The successes of the French prompted the U.S.Army aviation authorities to examine the feasibility of arming their helicopters.

A Typical Vertical Assault Scenario

A regiment in the Constantine area was ordered to sweep an area suspected of containing a band of eighty rebels. Because of the terrain, helicopter participation would be necessary. The operation was planned two days in advance. The helicopter annex of the operations order was based on the technical advice of the helicopter unit.

On the afternoon of the day before, the pilots of the four helicopters assigned to the mission gathered for a briefing with a representative of the fixed-wing SNJ squadron that was to furnish the initial air support. Maps were issued, studied and marked, together with aerial photographs of the landing site. The briefing, although informal, was thorough and precise.

The troops arrived by truck at the air base shortly before dawn the next morning. Upon disembarking, they were immediately formed into four helicopter teams of eight men each. Colored strips of cloth worn through their shoulder straps contrasted with their khaki green uniforms. This type of identification, modified on succeeding operations, was used to distinguish between friendly forces and rebel bands wearing captured uniforms. The embarkation in the warmed-up H-21s went smoothly. The troops made no effort to fasten their safety belts, which would have been difficult, if not impossible, in view of the hundreds of rounds of ammunition and hand grenades festooned about the cabin. Automatic weapons were distributed equally among the heliborne teams. Except for the portable communications equipment carried in the lead helicopter, neither the composition, equipment nor mission of any heliteam differed from that of any other.

Airborne thirty-five minutes before the drop, the troop-carrying helicopters were preceded to the area by fifteen minutes by a light reconnaissance aircraft. Its mission was to observe and report on conditions in the landing zone that could adversely affect the helicopter assault. Specifically, it was to report on the enemy's presence in the zone, and whether or not it received fire. Then two SNJ fixed-wing Scouts, orbiting out of sight, were called in for strafing runs by the observation pilot. At one minute before the planned helicopter landing, the observation pilot marked the landing zone with a smoke flare.

Control of the strafing aircraft was assigned to the pilot of the lead helicopter. With wind direction and velocity clearly indicated, he turned into his approach. The SNJs pulled up and orbited, ready to resume strafing at a moment's notice.

Thirty-two troops disembarked on a hilltop in a matter of minutes. In the valley below there were lines of troops—some stationary, others cautiously advancing. Behind them were the trucks that had brought them up the winding roads in the early morning hours. Overhead, the H-21s flew to a secondary pick-up zone where a truck-borne platoon of forty-eight stood waiting. This second lift required all four helicopters for the first run and a second trip by two of the helicopters. Upon completion of this lift, the helicopters utilized a shuttle racetrack pattern to immediately initiate a third lift of a rifle company to the landing zone. All possible avenues of escape in the objective area were now either occupied or covered by fire from the helicopter-borne troops commanding the ridge lines. Twelve minutes flying time away from the objective area, there was a clearing to which the helicopters withdrew to await possible on-call missions.[16]

A variation of this type of helicopter assault was known as "contact engagement." Less formal than the planned scenario, it was used when flexibility was paramount. When a rebel flare-up was reported, the helicopters were alerted and sent at maximum speed to the garrison nearest the action for a troop pickup. If relatively large rebel bands were involved, support aircraft and additional truck and helicopter-borne troops would immediately be dispatched to the area. The operation would then take the same form as a planned operation.[17]

Armor For Helicopters

If the helicopters were firing at the rebels, it followed that the rebels would fire back. This brought up the question of helicopter survivability in combat. The Army's view on the issue was clouded. They dealt with the problem with both tactics and hardware.

Early in the conflict, helicopter tactical evolution began with landing one or two helicopters almost directly upon the enemy. The rebels' inexperience with helicopters and weapons allowed such tactics to succeed. Helicopter casualties were relatively light in comparison to the number of combat hours flown, and it was believed that a realistic evaluation of helicopter vulnerability could be made on the basis of these losses. Subject to strafing and artillery fire, untrained in the intricacies of deflection shooting and often armed with a weapon better suited for clubbing, the effect of the rebel's fire was at first negligible. However, as the rebels gained experience, the French helicopters began to suffer an increase in the number of hits received.[18]

The resultant losses in men and equipment necessitated a re-examination of tactics. Steps to reduce vulnerability included the installation of self-sealing gas tanks on all H-21s. Armor plating was experimentally installed around certain engine components and the pilot's compartments (the pilots had long been wearing flak vests).[19] The armor was made of heavy fiberglass plastic and weighed a total of 30.8 pounds. It could stop a .30-caliber bullet unless it was fired at point blank range at zero degree incidence. A combination seat and groin shield was also developed to provide the pilots with additional protection. The seat was tied in place with straps to the seat support structure and the groin and vest parts were fastened to the pilot's body. The pilots reportedly did not care for the arrangement because it was too uncomfortable during long missions.[20]

No armor was used on the transmissions of the H-21s because of the desire to keep the weight to a minimum. No bullets were ever reported to have penetrated a transmission, and thus the danger was considered minimum.[21]

All of these efforts had a positive affect on helicopter vulnerability. Against .30-caliber fire, only one helicopter was lost for each 9250 hours of combat flying, although one was damaged by five or six hits in every 339 hours of combat flying. Even more significant is that the French did not lose any helicopters after employing suppressive and defensive weapons.

Lessons Learned

In terms of helicopter utilization in combat, the French accumulated a great deal of data and experience. Among the lessons learned were the following: having transport helicopters organic to the Army was better than having helicopter transport capability supplied by the Air Force; it was possible to maintain an availability of nearly eighty percent of all helicopters in combat; helicopter suppressive fire capability was absolutely necessary as it was successful in materially reducing combat losses; vulnerability of the helicopters to .30-caliber ground fire was considerably less than expected; the flight crews were the most vulnerable part of the helicopters and sustained more injury due to enemy fire than the troops carried; specialized helicopter training for highly trained troops was not required, nor was it required for untrained troops if they were brought in after the drop zone had been secured; a troop assault helicopter capable of carrying a minimum of thirteen troops to the highest and hottest existing conditions was desirable for the minimum troop "cell" employed; it was necessary in troop assault operations that a one and one-half ton payload helicopter be employed (again, capable of withstanding the highest altitude and greatest temperature); air support was superior to artillery support in helicopter troop assault operations; low-level "nap of the earth" flying in assault operations, although not employed in Algeria, was recognized as possibly being necessary against higher caliber ground fire and enemy air defenses; instrument flight capability was not practiced but desired; the turbine engine was superior to the reciprocating engine in combat and desert operating conditions; and pilots can fly over fifty hours per month in combat without undue medical or combat fatigue effects.[22]

The Algerian rebellion proved to be an important stepping stone for helicopter employment on the battlefield. It proved that helicopters could be configured with machine guns, rockets and antitank missiles, and could reliably support troops in the field. It was also the first combat employment of a helicopter equipped with turbo shaft engines—the Alouette II.

Vietnam: The Helicopter War

The Vietnam War was the spark that caused a virtual explosion in the use of combat helicopters and forced the marriage of weapons with modern rotary-wing aircraft. During no other time in history have so many kinds of helicopters been employed in battle than during this tragic war. Between the August 1964 congressional Tonkin Resolution and the January 1973 signing of the Paris Peace Pacts, no less than eighteen types of helicopters were flown by American aviators in Vietnam.*

This was the war that brought American weaponry up to the standard known as "high-technology," especially in the case of armed combat helicopters. Vietnam was the stage on which the first helicopter gunship, designed from the ground up, made its debut.

For many it is not possible to visualize scenes from the war without recalling the familiar Army helicopters—especially the familiar UH-1 Huey—and the characteristic thumping of their rotor blades. Rarely were there scenes where troops were marching into battle, as in World Wars I or II. The helicopter seemed to make Vietnam a "different kind of war."

One commentator said of helicopters in Vietnam,

> They were everywhere; day or night, rain or shine, good weather or bad; they were seen or heard every hour of the day. They hauled ash and trash; engaged in combat assaults; served as weapons platforms; scouted and flushed out enemy forces; transferred the wounded from forward medical aid facilities to rear area hospitals; and went into the thick of battle to evacuate the wounded to life-saving medical care. Army helicopters served as aerial artillery, and transported and repositioned whole gun crews, including ammunition. They were used to retrieve downed aircraft, and hauled tons of material and supplies—even beer and frozen pizza.[1]

These helicopters and their crews created a legacy that will be talked about for generations.

As was the British experience in Malaya, the United States could not have conducted ground operations in Vietnam without the helicopter. The terrain was ideal for a guerrilla war, and the Viet Cong and North Vietnamese took full advantage of it. The cover that the jungles offered and their knowledge of the land enhanced their ability to move and strike

---

*Specifically, the AH-1 Cobra, AH-1G Hueycobra, CH-21 Shawnee, CH-46 Sea Knight, CH-47 Chinook, CH-53 Sea Stallion, CH-54 Sky Crane (Tarhe), OH-13 Sioux, H-19B Chickasaw, H-23 Raven, CH-37 Mojave, HH-43 Huskie, OH-58A Kiowa, RH-53D Sea Stallion, SH-2 Sea Sprite, SH-3 Sea King, UH-1 Huey and the UH-34 Choctaw.

quickly. Therefore, helicopter mobility became an important, if not a vital, element of United States military operations in Southeast Asia.

The first helicopters used in Vietnam were the Sikorsky H-19B Chickasaws. These aircraft were flown by the French during the war against the Vietminh which lasted from 1946 to 1954, when the French signed the Geneva Accords. This ended the war and the French Indochinese state, and also established the seventeenth parallel demilitarized zone between the north and the south.

American commitment in the early stages of its involvement in Southeast Asia was limited to advising and training—mostly vested in the United States Military Assistance Advisory Group. But after the Tonkin Gulf Resolution, the United States' commitment was expanded to include combat elements. This was a particularly good time to employ helicopters because since the Korean War, the Army had been steadily increasing the number of aircraft it operated. In 1955, an expansion program was begun which increased the reliance upon helicopters as essential battlefield vehicles.

Between 1955 and the early 1960s, it became clear that the Viet Cong* planned to reunite North and South Vietnam by guerrilla warfare. The United States responded by building up South Vietnam's forces with conventional weapons and increasing advisory assistance.

The United States' involvement in Southeast Asia assumed large-scale proportions during the 1960s. This had great impact upon Army helicopter aviation. The number of Army aircraft in Vietnam grew from the original handful of Piasecki-built CH-21 Shawnee transport helicopters to approximately 4000 rotary and fixed-wing aircraft by 1971.[2] The basic missions fulfilled by helicopters in Vietnam included troop lift, aerial fire support, reconnaissance, logistical support and gunship operations.

The Vietnam War also served as the catalyst for the introduction of a new breed of combat helicopter: those built with the relatively new gas turbine engine which had an enormous power to weight ratio. This innovation in helicopter power plants was a major breakthrough that made rotary-wing aircraft better suited to combat operations. The introduction of the gas turbine engine marked the changeover from the smaller, slower, piston-engined helicopters that had been in service since the days of the Korean War.[3] The first helicopter equipped with the new engine was the UH-1A Huey, which has become symbolic of war itself.

Although designed and built by Bell as a light utility helicopter, the UH-1A served initially in Vietnam as an ambulance with the Fifty-Seventh Medical Detachment early in 1962. Later models would have a more powerful engine for greater cargo capability and provide for the installation of weapons, including four M-60 machine guns and mounts for sixteen 2.75-inch rockets. A test unit of UH-1A's was put together and sent to Thailand for maneuvers, and then deployed to Vietnam in September 1962.[4]

---

*Previously known as the Vietminh

Combat Helicopter Employment

One of the earliest initiatives involved helicopter support for the South Vietnamese Army supported by General Maxwell Taylor, then the Military Advisor to the President. He had the Eighth and Fifty-Seventh Transportation Companies ordered to Vietnam in 1961 for this purpose. The Eighth, located at Fort Bragg, North Carolina, was mobilized on November 20, 1961, and arrived at Qui Nhon in December with fifteen of its twenty authorized Piasecki CH-21 Shawnee transport helicopters. The Fifty-Seventh was ordered out of Fort Lewis, Washington on November 7, 1961. Its twenty CH-21s left Naval Station Alameda on November 21, 1961, followed by its two OH-13 light observation helicopters the following day. The movement was completed in May 1962.

In less than two weeks, the two units carried out the first heliborne combat operation of the Vietnam War, known as "Operation Chopper." During this operation, about one thousand South Vietnamese paratroopers were flown into what was thought to be a headquarters of the Viet Cong about ten miles west of Saigon. They did not meet the resistance they expected, but from the helicopter aspect the operation was successful.[5] Thus, helicopter aviation units were among the first of the United States' forces to arrive in and enter combat in Vietnam.

Many of the first helicopters used in Vietnam were leftovers from the Korean War. These included the two- and three-seated OH-13 Sioux and H-23 Raven helicopters, used for observation and reconnaissance, and the twin-rotor CH-21 troop transport. Later, the OH-58A Kiowa would replace the H-13s, while the H-23s and the CH-21s would be replaced by the UH-1 Huey, CH-53A Sea Stallion and the CH-46 Sea Knight.

The early workhorse was clearly the CH-21, built by Piasecki Aircraft, which carried approximately fifteen troops at 75 miles per hour. In service with the Army since 1954, it drew criticism in the early days of the Vietnam conflict for being underpowered and too slow,[6] making it a good target for ground fire from the Viet Cong. For example, an ARVN (Army of the Republic of Vietnam) heliborne operation was launched just before Christmas 1962 near Tuy Hoa in the II Corps Tactical Zone. Twenty-nine U.S. Army H-21's were committed to the operation without fixed-wing air support. The first three helicopters safely landed the Vietnamese troops, but six others were suddenly hit by fire from Viet Cong automatic weapons which caused many casualties. A U.S. Army company commander told a war correspondent that the casualties were caused by the fact that there had been no "softening-up" attack at the landing zone before the helicopters went in.[7]

Because the helicopter transports at the time did not always have escort firepower, they often had to provide their own. The CH-21 became one of the first helicopters configured with its own weapons. Ground fire suppression during troop landing operations was deemed a high priority because the Viet Cong were inflicting damage upon the H-21s. Accordingly, the CH-21s were configured with 30-caliber machine guns mounted in the door which were fired during landing operations. This measure was only marginally successful, however, because only one side of the aircraft was covered.

Helicopter combat tactics were untested and unproven. Some rather poorly coordinated strike operations during the early years of the Vietnam War led to the implementation of pre-mission combined briefings which included the helicopter transport flight leader, the helicopter gunship flight leader, the troop commander, the fixed-wing flight leader and the overall helicopter coordinator.[8] This coordination of airborne assets was a positive step toward improving landing zone (LZ) conditions.

Other steps were taken to improve the effectiveness of helicopter operations. Army and Air Force pilots often teamed up to search out the elusive Viet Cong. For example, UH-1B from the 118th Assault Helicopter Company (AHC) and a fixed wing Air Commando A-1E worked together as a hunter-killer team over the Mekong Delta in 1964.[9] Enemy ground fire also forced the helicopter transport pilots to improvise on their landing approaches and to invent some different patterns in the effort to reduce battle damage. Some patterns were successful, others were not.[10] Because these ad hoc efforts at developing tactics were of limited success, a special unit was created to develop combat helicopter tactics.

UTTHCO: Rotary-Wing Armed Escort

One of the first helicopter units to be organized and used in combat was the Utility Tactical Transport Helicopter Company (UTTHCO) assigned to the Forty-Fifth Transport Battalion. UTTHCO's mission was to furnish armed escort to the Thirty-Third, Fifty-Seventh and Ninty-Third Transport Companies. It was also directed to test the feasibility of providing armed helicopter escort for troop transport (Piasecki CH-21) helicopters, utilizing doctrine, tactics and techniques developed at the U.S. Army Aviation and U.S. Army Armor schools, in support of the Army of the Republic of Vietnam.[11]

On September 26, 1962 the commander of the U.S. Army, Ryukyu Island, directed the U.S. Army UTTH Company and its attached Twenty-Fifth Transportation Detachment to move to Tan Son Nhut, South Vietnam, where it was to establish its headquarters. The main platoon of six helicopters was at Quinhon.

This directive included the shipment of UTTHCO's fifteen new UH-1A single-engine turboshaft helicopters. The UH-1A's were equipped with two fixed 2.75-inch rocket pods each with eight tubes mounted on each skid. They could be fired in pairs, one on the left and one on the right. Additionally, they were configured on each side with two fixed forward-firing 30-caliber manually charged and electrically fired machine guns mounted on the skids. Flank and rear security was provided by door gunners armed with hand-held automatic weapons. Typically, some five thousand rounds of machine gun ammunition was carried.

UTTHCO flew its first combat mission on October 16, 1962. Soon after, as the data began accumulating, it became obvious that armed helicopters were successful at suppressing enemy small arms fire in the landing zones.

This was the beginning of the test period which ended the following March. The rules of engagement were simple: Targets could be engaged only when the unit's personnel and aircraft, or the transport helicopters, were fired on. Positive identification of the target location and the confirmed identification as Viet Cong must be made prior to engagement, the latter being made by an ARVN observer. One ARVN observer was required to be aboard each armed helicopter.[12]

The tactics developed during this test period varied according to the number of UH-1A's and UH-1B's being used because of their different capabilities.* The rocket-capable UH-1A's dominated the tactics during the first month of the evaluation. But the mix of weapons carried by the UH-1B's, it was determined, gave the unit commander greater flexibility when covering the LZ.

Early in the development phase, "Eagle Flights" were devised. These consisted of a hunter-killer team of typically four CH-21s carrying ARVN troops, three armed UH-1s and one observer for command and control (either an 0-1 or another UH-1) and a number of armed close air support T-28 Trojans. This formation was created to deal with insurgents escaping from ARVN ground sweeps. The airborne spotter attempted to locate the escapees and a nearby landing zone for the troop transports. The armed helicopter furnished escort for the transports and acted as a reconnaissance element.[13]

The presence of fixed-wing aircraft presented some problems. As more helicopters were being employed, more protection was needed during all phases of the missions. Accordingly, the Second Air Division commander was compelled to issue a regulation which standardized the procedure for fixed-wing fighters to escort helicopter transport formations. Usually, two fighters were involved in helicopter protection. One fighter would fly 'S' turns high and behind the formation. The other would fly low and ahead of the helicopters, executing 'S' turns in front of them, searching for enemy ground activity. The purpose of the low fighter was not necessarily to attack, but to suppress or draw fire away from the helicopters.[14]

Records indicate that by March 31, 1963, UTTHCO had flown 2075 hours of combat missions, of which 593 hours were service missions and 438 hours were for maintenance and training. UTTHCO fired some 44,000 machine gun rounds and 617 rockets that resulted in killing or wounding 153 insurgents.

The results of the evaluation were stunning, and favored armed

---

*The UH-1B compared to the UH-1A could carry eight instead of six passengers, lift 4000 as opposed to 3000 pounds external cargo and cruise at 90 instead of 80 knots. It was configured with a 40 mm grenade launcher, 7.62 mm machine guns, 2.75-inch rockets and M22 guided missiles.

helicopter escort of troop carrying helicopters. For each combat hour flown there was an immediate decrease in the number of helicopters hit by ground fire and in the number of total hits by ground fire. The number of hits received by transport helicopters decreased by one-fourth when they were escorted by armed helicopters,[15] although during this period the number of targets presented to ground fire and the potential for receiving such fire increased.[16]

The value of armed escort helicopters was further proven by the increased number of CH-21 "saves"; that is, helicopters that were downed by small arms fire, but were protected by the gunships until they could be repaired and flown out of the hot area. Four times CH-21s were effectively escorted and covered by UH-1s until they could be safely landed. Pilots confirmed that the amount of fire received by their units had decreased since the initiation of the armed helicopter escort.[17] Between October 16, 1962 and March 15, 1963 the unit flew almost eighteen hundred combat support hours and only one escort Huey was shot down.[18]

The Howze Board and Airmobility

By the early 1960s, the United States' military strategy had changed from its previous defensive posture of massive retaliation to a more flexible response to the Soviet threat. Beefed up conventional ground forces and mobility became an issue. Soon after taking office, Secretary of Defense Robert S. McNamara ordered a study of the conditions of Army mobility and asked for an estimate of the equipment needed to reach a satisfactory level. Not satisfied with the answers he got from this study, Secretary McNamara convened a powerful group of officers called the Army Tactical Mobility Requirements Board, commonly called the "Howze Board" out of respect for its chairman, General Hamilton H. Howze, a former Eighty-Second Airborne Division commanding general.[19]

The Howze Board was responsible for giving credibility to the concept of what has come to be known as "airmobility." The board consisted of fourteen generals, six high-ranking civilian research officials and more than thirty highly experienced but lower-ranking Army officers. Their mission was to study the role of Army aviation and its application to airmobility in its entirety. The secretary advised the board to give little regard to traditional military doctrine. General Howze was to study new organizational and operational concepts, possibly including completely airmobile infantry, artillery, antitank and reconnaissance units.[20]

The report to the secretary of defense was a masterpiece considering the limited time and resources. It recommended complete integration of airmobility into the Army field force structure, in balance with other tactical concepts. One of the most surprising recommendations was the substitution of aerial vehicles for large amounts of land transportation:

360 air vehicles for 2000 wheeled land vehicles.[21] In short, General Howze wanted to enhance the airmobility not only of infantry units, but also cavalry units, artillery units and logistical units.

The report also recommended that specialized, completely airmobile divisions be formed immediately. These divisions he called "air assault divisions." The combat troops belonging to them were to be 100 percent air-transportable, equipped with light, transportable weapons. Aircraft-mounted rockets would substitute for heavy artillery.

The recommendations eventually doubled the number of aircraft in the normal infantry division (from fifty to 101) and increased this number fourfold within the air assault divisions (459).

Secretary McNamara's initial response was to order a complete field test of the new concepts. For this he selected Major General W.O. Kinnard, an experienced and decorated parachute officer who had been interested from the beginning in the possible application of helicopters to infantry maneuvers.[22]

General Kinnard set up the skeleton of an air assault division at Fort Benning, Georgia with about 3000 men. Secretary McNamara requested authorization from Congress for an additional 15,000 men in fiscal year 1964 to complete the division. General Kinnard trained his officers and men from scratch. By January 1964, he had built his organization into two airmobile brigades of three battalions each and wanted to test them. He started maneuvering first with a battalion, then enlarged the test to accommodate a brigade. When he was satisfied that the concepts and techniques worked, he was ready to test the entire division.[23] "Air Assault II" was the last and most important test. It pitted General Kinnard's division against the Army's crack Eighty-Second Airborne Division in a leased maneuver area stretching from Fayetteville, North Carolina to Columbia, South Carolina. All concerned concluded that although the division was hindered by bad weather and vulnerable to tank attack, its mobility was characterized by a remarkably high tempo of operations and extremely short reaction time. It could fight in several directions at once, and over an unusually large area. Secretary McNamara was convinced.[24]

After three years of study, testing, field practice and evaluation, on June 16, 1965, the Secretary of Defense gave approval for the Army to proceed with the organization of an airmobile division as part of the active Army combat forces. The division selected for this honor was the famed First Cavalry Division and the test unit was the First Cavalry (Airmobile) Division. Eager to prove a point, the Army sent the division on its way to combat in Vietnam's highlands before the middle of the following month.

July 28, 1965 was an important day for the Army and for the acceptance of the helicopter into the airmobility concept. On that day, President Lyndon B. Johnson announced he had ordered the Air Mobile

Division to Vietnam: a "prototypical airmobile unit of the Second Division and the First Cavalry (Airmobile) Division." Major General Kinnard had been given only four weeks to get this new combat unit ready for the trip to Vietnam. On September 28, 1965 he announced that the division had closed into its An Khe base, two months to the day after the President's announcement. [25]

From then on, the Vietnam War accelerated the development of airmobility to a degree that would have seemed impossible a few years earlier. The American reliance on helicopters grew steadily. It is estimated that by January of 1966, the United States' forces had approximately one thousand helicopters in the war zone. Of these, no fewer than 428 aircraft belonged to the First Cavalry Airmobile Division. Appropriately dubbed the "Flying Horsemen," the 16,000-man division reached Vietnam in August and September 1965 as part of the American reinforcements. The First Cavalry was plainly one stage in the fulfillment of the air mobility concept, and its performance is sure to serve as an example for similar divisions in the future.[26]

The Boeing CH-47A Chinook and the Sikorsky CH-54 Sky Crane made important contributions to the Airmobility concept because of their enormous lifting capabilities. The CH-47A, for example, was a tandem rotor helicopter with two 2280 shaft horse power Lycoming T55-L-5 engines, which gave it the ability to lift more than 11,500 pounds.

Turbine Helicopter Gunships

High mobility was one of the two most important capabilities of the helicopter the war in Vietnam dramatized. The other was the true "gunship," the earliest of which was the UH-1B.

UTTHCO received the first of its twenty UH-1B's on November 24, 1962.[27] Although the UH-1s were not ideally suited for gunship missions, the advantages of the "B" model over the "A" were important to coping with the flying conditions helicopters are particularly sensitive to—high humidity and high density altitude weather conditions. Vietnam's weather was a constant problem because it reduced the performance of helicopters.

The UH-1A's 760-shp T53-L1A engines would only allow a maximum gross weight of 7200 pounds. The UH-1B's superior T53-L-9 1100-shp (a 45 percent power increase) engine increased the aircraft's maximum gross weight to 8500 pounds. The UH-1B helicopters had universal wiring and "hard points" for mounting three weapons systems. The first was the XM-6 quad, consisting of four M-60 7.62 mm machine guns, two mounted on each side, and 40 mm grenade launchers. They could be aimed remotely by the gunner in the cockpit or fired by the pilot when they were in the stowed position (pointing straight ahead). The second was the XM-3 rocket system which consisted of two pods mounted on each side, each containing twenty-four 2.75-inch rockets. The last was the SS-11 antitank guided missile system with three missiles externally-mounted on each side. As of the last day of December 1962, the later two were not available in South Vietnam.

This firepower now available to the commander in the field,

> highlighted the continuing controversy of tactical air versus armed helicopters in support of ground combat. Army commanders naturally considered armed helicopters more responsive to daily requirements than Air Force tactical fighter craft. But realizing the vulnerability of helicopters to heavy antiaircraft weapons and small portable missiles, Army officers regarded tactical aircraft and gunships as having their own respective places in any escalation of effort.[28]

The gunship provided light close-in fire support as an integral part of the ground force while the Air Force's tactical aircraft was considered best suited for heavy close air support and was not integrated into the ground forces.

As the war escalated in the mid-1960s, there was an increased need for heavy armaments. In the summer of 1966, the most heavily armed Army gunship in service was the UH-1B Huey gunship. However, this was a modified logistics helicopter, and at the time there seemed to be an obvious need for a dedicated helicopter gunship.

In 1966, after considerable testing and evaluation, the U.S. Army ordered the first true gunship, the AH-1 Huey Cobra. Equipped with one engine, the Cobra could accommodate a variety of weapons. For example, it could have two 7.62 mm miniguns or two M-129 40 mm grenade launchers mounted in a nose turret, and four M-157 or M-159 rocket launchers or two M-18E1 minigun pods slung under stubby wings on each side of the fuselage. It was highly maneuverable and presented a very small target when approaching head on.

The AH-1J was the first in a long line of Bell attack helicopters. The Bell AH-1T SuperCobra is still in use today. The AH-1G was a modified two-place version of the UH-1 designed as an armed gunship with the speed necessary to escort the troop-carrying CH-47 Chinook. The first Huey Cobras went to Vietnam in mid-l968.[29]

Marine Helicopter Support

Following the Korean War, the Marine Corps found itself much leaner than it wanted to be in terms of aircraft assets. It had less than 350 helicopters in service by 1962, 225 of which were UH-34D's. This venerable helicopter would be the mainstay for Marine Corps helicopter operations in Southeast Asia during the early years of the war.

Vietnam saw U.S. Marine Corps helicopters as early as April 1962 when the men of squadron HMM-362 established their base of operations eighty-five miles north of Saigon with twenty-four UH-34D's and a few light fixed-wing aircraft. This was the first phase of "Operation Shufly," the first U.S. Marine Corps helicopter troop and logistic support of the

South Vietnamese. Their mission was to provide battlefield airlift support. During these initial phases of "Shufly," it was learned that ground fire was a significant threat to safe operations, particularly in the landing zones. To deal with this problem, procedures were established to have weapon-configured Vietnamese T-28 Trojan trainers provide suppressive fire during landing zone operations.

During this period several Marine helicopter squadrons cycled in and out of Vietnam. By the late summer of 1962, HMM-362 had been relieved by HMM-163, which mounted M-60 machine guns and 7.62 mm miniguns on their UH-34s. They were directed to not fire unless fired upon.

HMM-162 arrived in early 1963 to relieve HMM-163. During its extensive combat experiences, HMM-162 also utilized M-60 machine guns while carrying out its missions, which included hauling everything from people to animals.

After having carved an airfield into the Vietnam countryside at Chu Lai (about fifty miles south of Da Nang) in the spring of 1965, the Marines brought in twenty-two Sikorsky UH-34D Choctaw helicopters belonging to squadrons HMM-361 and -261. These were used primarily for combat logistics under the watchful escort of armed UH-1E Huey gunships from Marine Observation Squadron (VMO) Two. The Hueys were configured with four M-60 machine guns and 2.75-inch rocket pods.

It is noteworthy that the UH-34 was still being flown as the Navy advanced helicopter training aircraft at Pensacola, Florida. With a maximum speed of 123 miles per hour, it could handle a payload of only 4900 pounds, and its days in combat were numbered.

The Marines finally replaced the tired single piston-engine UH-34D's with heavy-lift twin gas-turbine engine Sikorsky CH-53A Sea Stallions in 1967. Assigned to HMM-463, they increased the logistic capabilities of the Marine helicopter squadrons dramatically. The CH-53A was equipped with two General Electric T64-GE-6B turboshaft engines and had a payload capacity of more than 18,500 pounds—more than four times that of the UH-34. As a matter of fact, it could actually lift the UH-34.

The Marines also flew the CH-46 Sea Knight, assigned to HMM-164, which had arrived in Vietnam in the spring of 1966. The CH-46s had several accidents, but once the problems were corrected it served well for the remainder of the war. Still used today as a medium assault transport, the CH-46 is of the tandem-rotor configuration and was initially equipped with twin T-58-GE-10 engines.

A dramatic improvement to the Marine's helicopter firepower capability came in 1969 when the first true helicopter gunships—the Bell-built AH-1G Huey Cobras—arrived. These were the long-needed "light attack" helicopters that had the speed, maneuverability and firepower necessary to perform the troop transport escort mission. The Emerson TAT-101 nose-mounted gun turret gave "instantaneous fire suppression" power: one ingredient vital to helicopter escort missions.[30]

When South Vietnam finally crumbled under the onslaught of the North Vietnamese in early 1975, Marine Corps helicopters were there until the last minute. The CH-53 and CH-46 helicopters of HMH-462 and HMH-463 evacuated Americans from Saigon on April 29 and 30, 1975, during "Operation Frequent Wind." Among the approximately two thousand rescued was U.S. ambassador Graham Martin. This dramatic mission marked the end of the war for the United States.

The Air Force Air Rescue Service

January 10, 1962, marked the beginning of the U.S. Air Force's involvement with helicopter rescue operations in Southeast Asia. On that date, a hastily formed six-man advance team began organizing a "search and rescue (SAR) control center" at Tan Son Nhut. By April, this unit had been designated Pacific Air Rescue Center, Detachment Three. Even though the detachment had no aircraft assigned to it, it coordinated the use of Army and Marine Corps helicopters on SAR missions. Unfortunately, these assets proved to be only marginally successful for search and rescue missions.

Until a bonafide SAR helicopter could be designed and built, the Air Force flew the short-ranged HH-43 Husky. Even though it was poorly equipped for Vietnam rescue operations, it was used regularly and saved many lives. The Sikorsky CH-3 was also used for SAR during this period.

It was not until November 1965 that the first six Sikorsky HH-3E's—which came to be known as "Jolly Green Giants"—arrived in Vietnam. The HH-3E was a significantly modified CH-3, with many improvements that made it especially well suited for combat rescue. Its speed, endurance and ceiling of approximately ten thousand feet were about the same as the CH-3, but auxiliary fuel tanks increased its range to about 640 nautical miles. Operating out of Udorn, Thailand, or Da Nang, South Vietnam, it could reach any point in North Vietnam and still have enough fuel to return to its home base.[31] The introduction of the HH-3E was particularly timely as the number of calls for rescue missions was rising dramatically.

By 1967, the range of the HH-3E was further enhanced by inflight refueling using C-130 Hercules tankers. The first operational use of the aerial refueling technique involved an HH-3E helicopter, which had been assigned a Gulf of Tonkin orbit mission previously flown by the HU-16 (an amphibian fixed-wing aircraft). With the help of two mid-air refuelings by an HC-130P, the HH-3E flew the 8-hour mission, successfully demonstrating its improved range.[32]

In an effort to further improve its search and rescue capability, in 1967 the Air Force procured what came to be known as the Super Jolly Green Giant—the HH-53C. The advantages of this modified version of the Marine Corps CH-53A were that it could take thirty-eight passengers or twenty-four litters over 260 miles without auxiliary fuel tanks, protect itself with three 7.62 mm miniguns and fly at a speed of nearly 200 knots.

Night rescues were a problem for the SAR flight crews until 1971, when many of the HH-53C's were configured with low-light-level television equipment that allowed the pilots to "see" in the dark. A variety of other technologically advanced electronic devices were also installed in the aircraft that greatly aided in locating downed airmen.

The record of the Air Force rescue crews was remarkable. Between 1964 and mid-August 1973 they helped save 3883 lives. Of these, 2807 were U.S. military personnel: 926 Army, 680 Navy and 1201 Air Force. They also saved 555 allied military personnel, 476 civilians and 45 other unidentified persons. But they paid a high price: During the course of the war, seventy-one U.S. rescuemen were killed and forty-five aircraft destroyed.[33]

U.S. Navy Helicopters In Vietnam

In 1965 it was recognized that coastal and inner waterway patrol would be necessary to stop supplies for the Viet Cong from entering the country by water. The U.S. Navy was sent into action after the proposal was approved by the Joint Chiefs of Staff in March 1965. Given the code name "Market Place" under Task Force Seventy-One, the Navy took on the mission with surface ships and aircraft. Later in the year, control of the task force was turned over to General Westmoreland and the designation was changed to Task Force 115 with the code name "Market Time." Small river patrol boats (PBR's) were used, among other vehicles, for inner coastal river patrol and surveillance.

Support of the riverine forces became paramount early in the conflict. Captain John T. Shepherd, then assistant chief of staff for operations, U.S. Naval Forces Headquarters, Saigon, developed the idea of using U.S. Navy helicopter gunships to support the fast river patrol boats. Following this initiative, Detachment Twenty-Nine of Helicopter Combat Support Squadron (HC) One was formed in late June 1966 and arrived in Vietnam on July 4 with Lieutenant Commander William A. Rockwell, USN, as its officer-in-charge. In 1967, the combined detachments of HC-1 were brought together to form Helicopter Light Attack Squadron (HAL) Three, the first Navy attack squadron and the first squadron to be established in a combat zone. Flying UH-1B's and -1L's with flex-mounted .30-caliber machine guns and 2.75-inch rockets, the squadron routinely conducted aerial assault missions in support of the riverine forces. The "Seawolves" of HAL-3 flew up to twenty-two UH-1 Hueys and conducted operations from small land bases and landing ship transports (LSTs) in the Mekong Delta.

The Navy also provided helicopter search and rescue services in Vietnam. The "Big Mothers" of Helicopter Combat Support Squadron (HC) Seven were initially home ported at the Naval Air Station Atsugi,

Japan, and sent one- and two-helicopter detachments throughout the western theater. From the time it was established on September 1, 1967 to when it was disestablished on June 30, 1975 it provided search and rescue services from the Naval Air Stations at Atsugi and Cubi Point in the Philippines, vertical replenishment on various U.S. Navy ships, early minesweeping, and combat search and rescue in the Tonkin Gulf.

This was a composite squadron that flew Kaman-built UH-2B Sea Sprites for light logistics and combat SAR UH-46 Sea Knights for shipboard vertical replenishment, UH-34s for oceanographic research, HH-3A and SH-3G Sea Kings for combat SAR and RH-3A Sea Kings for mine countermeasures. All of these helicopters were capable of search and rescue.

In the combat SAR role, the HC-7 detachments would remain off the Vietnamese coast aboard Navy carriers.* Just one month after being established, the squadron's first rescue was carried out by Lieutenant Junior Grade Timothy S. Melecosy, pilot; Lieutenant Junior Grade James P. Brennan, copilot; Aviation Electrician Second Class Willie B. Pettit, first crewman; and Aviation Electronic Technician John H. Bevin, second crewman. While aboard the USS *Coontz* they were called to rescue Lieutenant Junior Grade Allan Perkins after he ejected from his aircraft in the Tonkin Gulf under small arms and 87 mm fire. This was the first of many daring rescue missions performed by the men of this unique squadron. Many of the rescues were inside North Vietnam, which earned the members of the outfit numerous decorations and the squadron the coveted Presidential Unit Citation.

During the Vietnam War, all Navy helicopter squadrons sent to the combat zone had at least a secondary mission of search and rescue (SAR). Every sortie flown could at a moment's notice be changed to combat SAR. Antisubmarine (ASW) helicopter squadrons which operated offshore in the Tonkin Gulf were routinely used for what was called "triple-S C," or SSSC for "surface and subsurface surveillance coordination." This meant that while on a routine logistics mission, the crews were responsible for conducting visual reconnaissance and reporting all surface craft activity. The SSSC mission was carried out on virtually every mission conducted from Yankee Station in the Tonkin Gulf even if the primary task only was moving mail between ships.

One ASW helicopter squadron in particular was tasked with not only maintaining antisubmarine warfare readiness but also with combat SAR on a regular basis as a bonafide mission. It was Helicopter Antisubmarine Squadron Two (HS-2), and it began carrying out this dangerous mission during its 1967 Western Pacific (WESTPAC) cruise. After extensive ASW training off the southern California coast in January and February 1967, HS-2 left its home port of San Diego, California on March 27 aboard the USS *Hornet*. Shortly after the squadron arrived at Pearl Harbor, a detachment dedicated to combat SAR was airlifted directly to Yankee

*The HC-7 detachments literally moved from one ship to another as they entered and departed Yankee Station in the Tonkin Gulf.

Station in the Tonkin Gulf and was assigned to the USS *Kitty Hawk* under the command of Task Force Seventy-Seven.

This detachment saw action almost immediately. On April 26, 1967, a "Big Mother" SH-3A piloted by Lieutenant Steve T. Millikin carried out a daring rescue by plucking Lieutenant J.W. Cain of VA-192 from inside Haiphong Harbor.

With the increase in the demand for helicopters, the Navy created the Assault Helicopter Office at the Naval Air Systems Command in 1968. Headed by Colonel K. L. Reusser, USMC, its mission was to bring together four helicopter programs—the CH-46, the CH-53, the UH-1 and the AH-1—with the Integrated Helicopter Avionics System (IHAS).[34]

In May of 1972, in the face of a major North Vietnamese offensive against the South, the United States mined North Vietnamese ports. Bombing continued until a ceasefire was established in January 1973 which included the release of American prisoners of war. The peace agreement called for the sweeping of mines. Accordingly, the initial staff of Task Force Seventy-Eight was established at Charleston, North Carolina. That same day, Helicopter Mine Countermeasures Squadron (HM) Twelve, which had been commissioned on April 1, 1971 and based at the Naval Air Station in Norfolk, Virginia, began loading its CH-53D helicopters and support equipment aboard Air Force C-5A transports for deployment to the western Pacific. Provision was also made for the use of Marine helicopters to augment the Navy's capabilities. Sea Stallions from HMH-463, stationed in Hawaii, joined the Navy teams arriving in the Philippines. This was the first time that United States naval aircraft would conduct aerial minesweeping in a live mine field.[35] Code named "Operation End Sweep," the operations were halted from time to time in order to keep POW release negotiations moving. Some 590 POW's were released by April 1, 1973, and Task Force Seventy-Eight completed its mission on July 27.

The Fall of the South

In January 1973, United States military operations ended in Vietnam and the final Peace agreement was signed. The following March, the last American troops left the country. Two years later, in the same month, North Vietnam launched a major conventional offensive against South Vietnam. In April of 1975, the South Vietnamese government crumbled and submitted to unconditional surrender. The last two U.S. sevicemen to die in Vietnam were helicopter crewmen—two Marines who were killed when their CH-53 crashed into the South China Sea.[36]

Top *The Soviet-built M-6 Hook is a true giant among military helicopters. It weighs 93,695 pounds fully loaded. When it was introduced in 1960, it was the largest helicopter in the world.* Tass.

Bottom *The Ka-25 Hormone has been used by the Soviet Navy since the 1960s as its principal ship-based helicopter.*

Opposite *The Soviet armed forces rely heavily upon the Mi-8 Hip. First produced in the early 1960s, it is used for assault missions, gunship operations, ambulance duties and minesweeping. It can transport up to twenty-eight passengers.*

Above *The Soviet Union's Mi-24 Hind was designed to operate in hostile environments. It was their first specialized helicopter gunship.*

Opposite *Among other things, the versatile and lightweight Soviet Mi-2 Hoplite has been a battlefield messenger and an observation platform. Its maximum gross weight is 8157 pounds.* UPI.

Top *The SH-3A Sea King was the basis for many other military and commercial models; some were used for assault, search and rescue, and minesweeping, as well as its original mission of ASW.*

Bottom *The West German entry into the attack helicopter market is the MBB BO 105 P. Here it is configured with six HOT antitank guided missiles. Many believe it to be the world's most maneuverable helicopter due to its hingeless rotor system and fiberglass rotor blades.* Messerschmitt-Bolkow-Blohm GmbH.

07
NAVY

Opposite *A U.S. Navy UH-46 Sea Knight utility helicopter on board a British carrier in 1972.*

Top *This Aerospatiale SA 342 L1 Gazelle is firing a HOT antitank missile. It can carry up to six of these missiles for battlefield missions.* Aerospatiale.

Bottom *The twin-turbined French-built Aerospatiale SA 365 M Panther's missions include day and night anti-tank using up to eight HOT missiles, and fire support with 20 mm pod-mounted cannons and rockets. It can also carry up to ten commandos.* Aerospatiale.

Top *UH-1 helicopters from the 52nd Aviation Battalion stop for refueling in Wonju, Korea.* U.S. Army.
Bottom *The H-1 series, usually called the Cobra, was built in 1966 for the U.S. Army.* Bell Helicopter Textron.

Opposite:
Top *This Aerospatiale AS 332 F1 Super Puma is shown with two AM 39 Exocet missiles.* Aerospatiale.
Center *A U.S. Air Force HH-60A Night Hawk.* Sikorsky Aircraft.
Bottom *The U.S. Navy is currently deploying the Sikorsky-built SH-60B Seahawk, which is equipped with surface search radar, magnetic anomaly detection, sonar bouys, ship-to-aircraft data link systems and homing torpedoes.* Sikorsky Aircraft.

NAVY

Opposite:
Top *The AH-64 Apache carries sixteen Hellfire missiles for the antitank role.*
Center *Here it is shown firing rockets during tests.* Hughes Helicopters.
Bottom and above *The CH-53E Super Stallion is capable of lifting sixteen tons, giving it the greatest lift capacity of any helicopter in the West.*

Following page *The RH-53D Sea Stallions of HM-16 perform airborne mine countermeasures. These twin-engined helicopters can sweep mines more quickly and safely than surface minesweepers.*

635

836
836

Previous page *The CH-47 Chinook is a medium-lift transfer helicopter used by many countries, including the U.S. Here, U.S. Marines are boarding a CH-47 during joint service exercise Solid Shield 79.*

Above *Two CH-58 Kiowa Scout helicopters followed by four UH-60 Blackhawk utility helicopters and two AH-1S Cobra attack helicopters fly over the pyramids outside of Cairo.*

Developments in the Soviet Union

The Soviet Union was involved in practical helicopter development long before the Western world. Indeed, the United States' premier helicopter design is attributable to a Russian-born immigrant, Igor Sikorsky.

The Soviet Union's military and civilian helicopter inventory today can be safely termed the largest fleet of the most heavily armed rotary-wing aircraft in the world. What they lack in electronic and engineering sophistication, they make up for in numbers and lifting capabilities.

Russia's history of rotary-wing development goes back many years. Approximately three centuries after Leonardo da Vinci sketched his famous "air screw" in late 1400s, a Russian by the name of Boris Yuriev was writing his treatise, "The Aerodynamic Design of Helicopters," a major scholarly work of the period. In 1754, a brilliant Russian scholar and scientist, Mikhail Lomonosov, built a working model of an "air screw." Following him were several helicopter design pioneers who brought the Soviet Union to its prominence today in helicopter development. The list includes A.N. Lodygen in 1869, I. Bykov in 1897, Konstantin Antonov in 1907, N. I. Sorokin and V.V. Tatarinov in 1909, Nikolai I. Kamov in 1929, Alexksandr Yakovlev of the 1940s and Mikhail Mil in the 1950s.

The evolution of Soviet military helicopters has been a gradual, low-risk progression of helicopter designs, each clearly expressive of the attitude of the military toward helicopter use in combat. They have gone the full course from small utility helicopters with snap-on machine guns to today's sophisticated assault helicopters equipped with rockets, missiles, electronic sensors and targeting devices, and automatic machine guns.

Rotorcraft development began in the Soviet Union in much the same way as it did in the United States. The Soviets' first rotary-wing aircraft was an autogiro, the Kaskr-I, designed and built by N.I. Kamov and N.K. Shrzhinsky in 1929. It was virtually a replica of the Cierva C.8 autogiro, and the first of several autogiros built in the Soviet Union.

Unlike the United States, whose autogiro military experiments focused on logistics, reconnaissance and battlefield spotting, the Soviets wasted no time in experimenting with mounting machine guns on their autogiros. The TsAGI A-7 was studied by the Soviet Army and evaluated with a nose mounted synchronized ShKAS 7.62 mm machine gun. Although the experiments did not show a great deal of promise, the TsAGI was used during World War II by the Soviet Union Air Force near Smolensk in 1942.

During the mid-1940s, true helicopter designs took shape under Aleksandr Yakovlev's group which fabricated a small coaxial-rotor single-engine system. Although it flew, it never achieved production or earned the status of being assigned a name.[1]

The Soviet Union's first few helicopters were not very original in design or appearance. The first three were very similar to western helicopters. In 1947, a prototype single-rotor, single-engine helicopter called the Yak-100 appeared. It was a virtual replica of the Sikorsky S-51,* which the United States armed forces flew so gallantly and with great success in the Korean war. It was extensively tested and ready for state acceptance in 1950, but it was too late because the Mi-1 had already been selected for full production.[2]

The Mi-1 Hare, a four-place, single engine, single-rotor helicopter was also introduced during the late 1940s. It bore a striking resemblance to the British-built Bristol Sycamore, but demonstrated poorer performance. Produced in large numbers (between two and four thousand) it was primarily used for military transport and communications.

In the early 1950s, the Soviets introduced the Mi-4 Hound, which resembled the Sikorsky H-19 in both appearance and performance. They built a large number of Hounds for medium-lift in military logistics, land-based antisubmarine warfare and civilian transport. They were capable of carrying ASW sensors, depth charges and rockets.[3] Production of the Mi-4 continued long after the United States discontinued building the H-19s. In fact, it is still widely used for military and civil purposes. The Hound-A is the military version while the "B" model is the naval version. It was configured with 12.7 mm manually trained machine guns to be used for defense.

The next significant helicopter with military potential to be produced in the Soviet Union was the Ka-26 Hoodlum in 1965. Still in use today, primarily in the medium lift mission, it has twin radial engines, coaxial-rotors and a maximum lift of approximately 7165 pounds.[4] It is produced primarily for commercial use—light logistics and crop dusting.

The Soviet Union's realization of the cargo carrying potential of the helicopter became obvious during the late 1950s. Sheer size became the innovation in the Soviet Union's helicopter development when in 1957 the Mi-6 Hook appeared. This five-bladed, single-rotor giant helicopter has two 5500 shaft horse power turbines with a maximum gross weight of more than 93,695 pounds—some 20,695 pounds more than the largest helicopter in the west, the United States' CH-53E Super Stallion. Showing major innovations in helicopter technology, it was Russia's first turbine powered helicopter. Used primarily for tactical assault missions,

*The Sikorsky S-51 was also designated the R-5, H-5, HO2S, HO3S, and the Dragonfly.

it is primarily a troop carrier and logistics support aircraft. Today it is flown principally by Peru, Bulgaria, Iraq, Syria, Indonesia and Vietnam.

In the early 1960s, the Soviets showed a great deal of interest in applying helicopters to antisubmarine and antisurface warfare, by integrating them with their mighty surface fleet. The 1961 appearance of a prototype known as the Ka-20 Harp showed great imagination and impressive use of available technology. The coaxial-rotor Harp used gas turbines for the first time, could carry air-to-surface rockets and machine guns, and was fitted with radar. In 1968, the Ka-20 eventually evolved into what is known today as the Ka-25 Hormone, the backbone of the Soviet Union's antisubmarine helicopter fleet.

The Hormone's appearance also brought the helicopter and the surface ship together and combined their relative strengths: the staying power of the *Kresta I* cruiser (the first Russian surface combatant to be constructed with a helicopter landing area and hangar) and the short-range speed of the helicopter. This is a concept known in the United States as LAMPS—Light Airborne Multi-Purpose System. The Hormone, configured only with torpedoes and depth bombs, supported not only its original antisurface mission with over the horizon targeting, but also its new role in antisubmarine warfare.

The Hormone also appeared on the first Soviet aviation ships classed as "ASW cruisers": the 18,000-ton *Moskva* in 1967 and, two years later, the *Leningrad.* It also appeared on the much larger angle-decked *Kiev* antisubmarine cruiser in 1975. The *Kiev* also included for the first time another vertical-flight capable aircraft, the fixed wing Yak-36 Forger fighters.

An improvement of the Ka-25 Hormone appeared for the first time in early February 1982. Designated the Ka-32 Helix, its engine and transmission compartments and the "chin bubble" are slightly different, which suggests an upgraded engine and a different radar. The Helix is also configured with Magnetic Anomaly Detection (MAD) equipment, and is designed to operate from the decks of Soviet destroyers.

In the early 1960s the West witnessed the introduction of an armed Russian helicopter with a great deal of combat versatility. The Mi-8 Hip, first flown in 1962, is a single-rotor twin-turbine logistics helicopter that can not only carry up to eleven passengers, but in its "C" version can be configured with four 16-shot 57 mm rocket pods, four 250 kilogram bombs or two 500 kilogram bombs, and a light machine gun mounted in the door. It was also designed to allow the infantrymen passengers to fire their personal weapons from the aircraft through the windows. The "E" and "F" variants are armed with six Sagger anti-armor missiles used in battlefield combat support. In 1981 an improved version appeared designated the Mi-17. It is an armed cargo helicopter. Manufactured in great numbers, it is flown by more than twenty-nine nations.

Another variation of the Hip that appeared in the mid-1970s was the

Mi-14 Haze. Used primarily for shore-based antisubmarine warfare (ASW) for the Soviet Naval Air Force (AV-MF), it has the capability of performing mine countermeasures. Single-barrelled machine guns were mounted in Mi-4 Hip-C's and Hip-E's. They also have rockets to provide suppressive fire during the assault phase of operations, capitalizing on the experience of France and the United States.[5] The Mi-4s are also often seen carrying four 57 mm rocket pods. They are currently being flown by Libya, Syria, Bulgaria, East Germany and Cuba.

The Mi-14 Haze-A, flown by Russia, East Germany and Poland, is the ASW version of the Hip-C with dipping sonar and magnetic anomaly detection sensors. The "B" version is used for mine countermeasures by towing a mine sweeping sled.

The changing attitude of Soviet military leaders showed an extraordinary shift in the 1970s toward increasing the involvement of heavily armed helicopters in combat operations. In 1972 they introduced the Mi-24 Hind-A, the first in a series of heavily armed attack helicopters. It is fast, agile, loaded with weapons and can still carry combat cargo. It is believed to be designed to provide its own fire cover while inserting assault troops in a combat landing zone. It is a five-bladed single-rotor twin-turbine helicopter with a maximum gross weight of 22,046 pounds. It is configured with a machine gun, four antiarmor missiles and rockets which are mounted on small stub wings amidship on each side of the fuselage.

This helicopter is still not a pure gunship. Influential members of the Soviet staff at the time argued that the aircraft must be designed with a cargo bay for logistical applications, because they could not afford a sophisticated single-purpose helicopter in such great numbers.[6]

As Soviet attitudes changed, the Hind went through several metamorphoses, each an improvement over the last. The Hind-D demonstrated the most dramatic changes, with a new nose configuration housing a Gatling-type gun and an optical sensor system. The Hind-E, introduced in 1976, was outfitted with antiarmor missiles mounted on the small stubby winglets and was capable of carrying up to ten troops. One curious thing about the evolution of this remarkable helicopter is that on the "A" and "B" models the tail rotor is mounted on the starboard (right) side of the fuselage, while on the "C" and later models it is mounted on the port (left) side.

In the area of heavy lifters in the Soviet Union, there is the Mi-26 Halo which was first seen by western observers in 1977. Truly a giant among rotary-wing aircraft, it is indisputably the heaviest helicopter in the world. This eight-bladed, single-rotor, twin-turbine giant weighs 109,128 pounds. It made its first public appearance east of the Iron Curtain at the Paris Air Show in 1981, and was seen again at the Farnborough Air Show in England in September 1984. So far it does not seem to be configured with weapons. Used primarily for logistics, it is expected to see great military service with time.

The growth and development of helicopter aviation in the Russian armed forces has been impressive. Within five years their force levels have approximately doubled, increasing from some 400 attack helicopters in 1978 to approximately 800 by 1983. Along the way, they have established Army aviation and integrated helicopters into the divisional assets of their field forces.[7]

Armed Soviet helicopters have evolved a great deal during the past thirty years. Their weapons systems have become so effective they appear to be slowly replacing fixed-wing aircraft in the area of close air support for ground forces.

Soviet armed helicopter units allocate part of their weapons training to bombing operations.[8] When their helicopter assets are combined to form combat units, their capabilities become formidable. Consider the Hind with four antitank guided missiles, one hundred and twenty-eight 57 mm rockets, four bombs, four pod mounted guns, a 23 mm radar-directed gun turret and up to a dozen troops teamed with a Hook with sixty-five troops and you have a fast moving, flexible combat unit able to go virtually anywhere it wants to.[9]

Russian helicopters seem to be relatively par with those of the United States in terms of their night and instrument flying capabilities. Russian tactical forces are well equipped for night operations with infrared search lights, thermal imagers and automatic navigational systems. Night combat capability gives the advantage of being able to select the time and the place of the strike. This was clearly demonstrated in Czechoslovakia in 1968 on the night of August 20, when the Soviets set down troops throughout the country to stop the Dubec liberalization tendencies.[10]

Tactics

The Russians have clearly planned for their helicopter assets to be used to achieve decisive results in combat. Their tactics emphasize speed, mobility and firepower, and the helicopter is well suited to this scenario. The Soviets have given a great deal of attention to utilizing every versatility the helicopter affords.

Their modern tactics call for simultaneous attack of enemy positions in depth, utilizing surface and air elements in which the assault helicopter plays a significant role. The Hind, for example, can be used either in independent helicopter regiments under the control of the front commander or as support for ground forces, which includes command and control, reconnaissance, logistics and electronic warfare.[11] They are also configured to counter air threats with the use of cannons and infrared-sensor missiles.

Specifically, Soviet motorized rifle and tank divisions now have organic helicopter squadrons assigned. Typically the squadrons have eighteen aircraft and two hundred personnel. Squadron-sized units with six Hind, six Hip and six Hoplite aircraft have been incorporated into the motorized rifle and tank divisions to create a force structure which gives the division commander a remarkable degree of flexibility. Furthermore, the independent assault helicopter regiments (IAHR) are a vital part of the Soviet Armed Forces' "new" operational concepts—the operational maneuver groups (OMG) and the airmobile/air assault brigades (AAB).

Early in an engagement, the OMG and the AAB (with fifty to sixty helicopters) would be dispatched quickly to the rear of the enemy's defensive formations. It is estimated that about 350 Hind D's and E's (out of approximately one thousand built so far) are stationed in East Germany and Czechoslovakia.[12]

These combat tactics have surely been influenced by the Soviets' observation of the successful use of assault helicopters by the United States and the United Kingdom. For a long time the Soviet Union's military leaders were not convinced of the helicopter's value in combat. That skepticism prevailed until they observed the U.S. Army's armament developments during the 1950s and their successful employment of helicopters in Vietnam. Most recently, Russian publications have indicated that Soviet military leaders have also learned from the Falkland War. Addressing the fighting on East Falkland Island, one article noted, "The decisive (factor) in combat operations to take possession of the Falkland Islands turned out to be conducting the assault operations using a large number of helicopters." Another journal stated that, "Without the support of these helicopters, the combat operations ashore would not have been so successful and so promptly executed."[13]

Russian Helicopters In Afghanistan

While the western world was enjoying the Christmas holiday in 1979, the Soviet Union invaded Afghanistan. According to newspaper reports, a motorized rifle division of about twelve thousand troops moved into Kandahar from the Russian city of Kushka. Others poured in from Termez and overran the cities of Bagrāmē and Kabul. By mid-January it was a full-blown invasion of some 75,000 troops.

President Hafizullah Amin was ousted and executed immediately. Babrak Kamal was quickly installed as the new President and Secretary General of the ruling People's Democratic Party and a puppet for the Soviet Union.

To defend themselves from the onslaught, the Afghan resistance turned to guerrilla warfare. The Russians countered with more ground troops and armed helicopters.

As of January 1983 it was estimated that between 500 and 600 helicopters were deployed to Afghanistan; nearly 200 of these were heavily armed Mi-24 Hind gunships to support some 105,000 Soviet troops. By late 1986, it was estimated that the Russians had lost at least 100 Mi-24s during the fighting.[14]

The Afghan guerrillas enjoyed the same advantages as the rebels during the French-Algerian War—knowledge of the language, culture, terrain and the will to fight—and the Soviets hoped to neutralize these advantages with helicopter gunships. To date, the Russians' success appears to have been only marginal.

The helicopter tactics employed by the Soviets in Afghanistan are very similar to those used by the United States in Vietnam. The Soviet command selects an area of guerrilla activity, then the combat troops are transported by helicopter and once on the ground, supported by Mi-24 gunships.[15]

The Russians use their armed helicopters for close air support, antiarmor, antihelicopter, commando, transport of antitank units, heliborne escort and armed rescue missions. The United States government has reported that the 1200 Russian Hind and Hip helicopters are equipped for chemical warfare.[16] There have been reports of chemical warfare being used against the Mujadeen resistance in Afganistan.[17]

The war in Afghanistan continues with only sketchy reports released. Each report, however, relates extensive utilization of the Soviet Union's latest combat helicopters. This indicates that the helicopter has earned a respected place in the minds of Soviet military planners.

The Afghanistan invasion marks the Soviet Union's first direct use of helicopters in combat. Regardless of their success or failure in Afghanistan, they are gaining a great deal of valuable experience.

Fighting Helicopters of the 1980s

The Soviet Union's invasion of Afghanistan continues to be the longest war employing helicopter gunships since Vietnam. The conflict doesn't seem to be near resolution as Russian troops continue to be harassed by Afghan guerrillas. An accurate, in-depth discussion of helicopter operations in Afghanistan is not possible because there is a lack of reliable information.

However, helicopters were used in combat in two other small wars during the first half of this decade. They were the Falkland Islands War in the southern portion of the Atlantic Ocean (during which the British successfully regained possession of the islands from Argentina) and the United States' rescue mission on the island nation of Grenada in the Caribbean Sea. Both operations serve as excellent examples of how rotary-wing aircraft can significantly enhance the speed and flexibility of amphibious military operations. The Falkland Islands War is especially interesting because, thanks to state of the art missile technology, it opened the door to a new helicopter mission—antiship warfare.

These military confrontations, as short as they were, deserve close examination in terms of the successful use of rotary-wing aircraft. However, the 1980s began with a demonstration of the risks involved in using these increasingly versatile machines.

The Iranian Rescue Mission

On November 4, 1979, Iranian students seized the American Embassy in Tehran. The nearly six months of preparations preceding the April 1980 attempt to rescue the fifty-two American hostages held by the fundamentalist government of the Ayatollah Khomeini was carried out under an impenetrable cloak of secrecy. In contrast to this, the mechanical failures of three of the helicopters involved in the attempted rescue was exposed to glaring public examination.

The mission began with the launch of eight RH-53D Sea Stallion helicopters from the flight deck of the USS *Nimitz* in the Gulf of Oman at 7:30 P.M. local time on April 24, 1980. The helicopters belonged to Helicopter Mine Countermeasures Squadron Sixteen (HM-16), home based at the Naval Air Station in Norfolk, Virginia, and were reconfigured with the latest state-of-the-art electronic systems. These included

OMEGA and inertial navigation systems, visual navigational equipment and night vision devices. These helicopters were the best available for this type of mission because of their long endurance and heavy lifting capacity. Their presence in the Gulf of Oman was understandable, and therefore unsuspicious to any observers, because their mine sweeping capabilities might be used in the event the Strait of Hormuz was mined. This coordinated effort also included six C-130 Hercules transport aircraft which were flown from a base in Egypt to rendezvous with the helicopter flight. The C-130s carried supplies, fuel and ninety commandoes.

The destination of the helicopters was Dasht-i-Kavir, designated "Desert One," approximately 250 miles southeast of Tehran and some 600 miles inland. There they were to set up a temporary staging base for refueling and final preparations before going to Tehran.

Only two hours into the mission, the Number Six RH-53D made an emergency landing due to an indication of imminent rotor blade failure.* The helicopter was abandoned and the crew continued with its classified materials to Desert One aboard helicopter Number Eight, which quickly caught up with the rest of the formation.

Approximately an hour after the loss of Number Six, the flight encountered an unforcasted, severe dust storm, known as a "haboobs," which significantly reduced visibility. While attempting to fly through the dust storm, helicopter Number Five lost its gyro (artificial horizon) which is the primary instrument used in poor visibility. The pilot decided to abort and returned to the *Nimitz*.

The remaining six helicopters continued on to Desert One and arrived approximately one hour and twenty-five minutes later than planned. The Number Two helicopter was grounded upon arrival due to a partial hydraulic failure of the flight control systems. The decision to terminate the mission if less than six helicopters were available had already been made. President Jimmy Carter in Washington reaffirmed this difficult choice, and the flight was ordered to abort.

While one of the remaining helicopters was being repositioned for refueling in the dark and noise-engulfed desert site, its rotor blades contacted one of the fuel-laden C-130 transports. They were both immediately consumed in flames, causing the death of eight crew members and injuries to five more.

The malfunction of the three helicopters' subsystems was most likely due to chance. Every possible precaution to prevent system failures was used. The extensive pre-maintenance performed on all eight aircraft included numerous special maintenance procedures, and special supply support was also provided. The post-mission investigation revealed that the main rotor blade and hydraulic malfunctions were due to material failures. The gyro malfunction occurred because a cooling blower that fed the gyro system was blocked by equipment stowed inside the cabin of the

*The RH-53D main rotor blades are configured with a blade integrity warning system (BIM) which alerts the pilots to a high probability of failure.

helicopter. Never before in the history of rotary-wing operations has every detail of a helicopter operation been so exposed to world-wide public view and investigated so carefully.

The Falkland Islands War

It started with a small military action by the Argentine forces: They attacked and captured the British Royal Marine's garrison on the Falkland Islands one spring morning in 1982. It quickly turned into a bloody seventy-four day war with the British the victors. The Argentine government and military leaders had underestimated the resolve of the British, and they paid dearly for it.

The Falkland Islands War proved many things; among them, that technology has a place on the battlefield. The war reaffirmed that soldiers with the "right stuff" and the right equipment were a winning combination. It also proved that missile technology, in this case the French-made Exocet AM39 missile, could reap great harm on the enemy at relatively little cost. These missiles caused significant damage to two British ships and sank the destroyer *Sheffield* and a container ship, the *Atlantic Conveyor*.

This war also demonstrated that the vertical takeoff and landing strike/fighter could perform beyond expectations, and that the helicopter was indispensable to modern warfare. Overall, more than 170 helicopters were used in the fighting.

Located in the South Atlantic, the Falkland Islands have been a source of conflict since their discovery in the sixteenth century. Depending upon who you read, the islands were first discovered either by a Portuguese pilot from Magellan's 1520 expedition, or by the English navigator John Davys who claimed them for the crown in 1592. The islands changed hands a few times until 1833, when the British established a permanent colony, using force to remove the Argentine settlement.

Argentina continued to claim the islands, which include South Georgia, South Sandwich, South Orkney and South Shetland. Their location, some 300 miles east of the Straits of Magellan, do have strategic value. The islands' terrain and climate are very similar to the Orkney Islands off the coast of Northern Scotland.

On April 2, 1982, Argentina decided to take its long-term claim to the islands seriously and invaded Port Stanley and, the next day, South Georgia. Three days later, amid a cheering crowd, the main part of a British task force set sail from the United Kingdom. Its mission was to use whatever force necessary to regain the islands under the code name "Operation Corporate."

The Fleet Air Arm had to pool its resources in order to combine flexibility, mobility, surprise and quick reaction. The Royal Navy's carriers fitted into the scenario well; The carrier group included Rear

Admiral J.F. Woodward's flagship, the 25,000-ton HMS *Hermes,* with twelve Sea Harriers of Squadron Number 800 and fifteen Westland Sea King antisubmarine warfare helicopters of Squadron Number 826. Also included were the 16,500-ton HMS *Invincible,* with eight Sea Harriers of Squadron Number 801 and nine ASW Sea Kings of Squadron Number 820, the frigates *Alacrity* and *Antelope* and the Royal Fleet Auxiliary's *Almeda* and *Resource.* The HMS *Hermes* later received nine more Sea Kings configured for combat support from Squadron Number 846, which were used to support Royal Marine commando operations.

After the carriers were on their way, the Fleet Air Arm Squadrons Number 848 (with twelve Wessex-5s), Number 847 (with sixteen Wessex-5s), and the Number 825 (with ten Sea King-2s) were established before the third of May. Royal Air Force Squadron Number 18, with five Chinooks (heavy transport helicopters) was also added to the task group. Squadrons Number 848 and 18 were placed aboard the *Atlantic Conveyor,* a commercial container ship, for the trip south. At ascension they were joined by the Fleet Air Arm's (FAA) Squadron Number 809's Sea Harriers and the Royal Air Force's (RAF) Squadron Number 1's modified Harrier GR-3s. Squadrons 847 and 825 departed on the RFA *Engladine* and the *Atlantic Causeway* in May. The Carrier Group was joined in the combat area by the guided-missile frigate HMS *Brilliant* with two Lynx helicopters.

On the morning of April 21, a Wessex-3 helicopter was launched from HMS *Antrim* to scout the area in the vicinity of Leith and Stromness, Saint Georges. Finding the conditions marginally satisfactory, it and two other Wessex-5s, from HMS *Tidespring,* transported Special Air Service Regiment commandos to the Fortuna Glacier in blinding snow (after two attempts). The following day, the commandos had to be retrieved in freezing "white out" flying conditions. The result was two Wessex crashes.

The first hostile engagement with the enemy involved the sinking of an Argentine submarine. On April 25, a British Fleet Air Arm Wessex-3 from HMS *Antrim* dropped two forty-year-old Mk-11 depth charges next to the Argentine Guppy II-class submarine *Santa Fe,* which forced the already surfaced submarine to make a run for Grytviken. Then a Wasp helicopter from HMS *Endurance* fired an AS-12 wire-guided missile through the submarine's sail, adding to the damage. The HMS *Brilliant*'s Lynx dropped a torpedo and harassed her with machine gun fire. The combined helicopter attacks caused sufficient damage that the *Santa Fe* beached herself near Grytviken and later sank.[1]

On April 30 the Total Exclusion Zone, within which any Argentine was considered a risk, was announced. Meanwhile, the *Hermes'* Sea Kings conducted continuous ASW operations out to twelve miles from the task force while extensive air-to-air Harrier combat was being conducted overhead. Other helicopters conducted surface and search surveillance out to 200 miles.

The Sea Kings, for the first time in actual combat conditions, extended their area of operations by conducting inflight refueling from frigates far from the main task group. This procedure allows the helicopter to hover just off one side of the ship's fantail while taking on fuel through a hose.

During that same time, helicopters from the ships *Antrim, Tidespring, Endurance* and *Brilliant* participated in landing troops ashore, bombardment spotting and ship-to-shore logistics.

There is one interesting story that demonstrates the flexibility of the helicopter in combat. When the HMS *Sheffield* was hit by an Exocet missile on May 4, the *Yarmouth* was in the vicinity and went to her aid. The Wasp helicopter's role was changed to Verticle Replenishment and Casualty Evacuation. It ferried extra fire-fighting equipment to, and survivors from, the stricken destroyer, landing on the burning ship several times. While the *Yarmouth* was alongside the *Sheffield,* taking off survivors, she came under torpedo attack. The *Yarmouth* broke off to use mortars, and the Wasp was subsequently recalled to change its mission to ASW. It was launched with two torpedoes to assist the ship and joining "dippers" (ASW helicopters) in submarine prosecution. One torpedo was dropped by the Wasp.[2]

Air-to-surface missiles carried on helicopters were used for the first time on May 3. The scenario began on May 2, when two Lynx helicopters, one each from the destroyers *Glasgow* and *Coventry* were sent in search of two Argentinean patrol boats, A69 corvettes, believed to be operating in the Total Exclusion Zone. The following day, *Coventry's* Lynx picked up a contact, after which an HMS *Invincible* Sea King intercepted and fired on contact. The Lynx was then called in to attack the vessel with two Sea Skua missiles. They both hit the target, which was later identified as the *Commodore Somellera.* She exploded with a spectacular flash that could be seen miles away. Sea Skuas were used successfully again on May 16, when a Lynx from Antelope Flight attacked and sank the Argentine merchant ship *Rio Carcarana.*

Lynx helicopters routinely conducted aerial artillery spotting and were often picked up by enemy fire control radar. At one point, a Lynx helicopter engaged an Argentine patrol boat with machine gun fire.

On May 9, Squadron Number 800's Sea Harriers conducted a successful strike against an Argentine intelligence-gathering trawler. The Sea King-4s of Squadron Number 846 were launched to transport the boarding party to the trawler.

The first landing party raid by the Special Forces took place on May 15, supported by Squadron Number 846's Sea Kings at Pebble Island. The mission resulted in the destruction of several aircraft, including six Pucaras.

All during the Commando Brigade landing at San Carlos on May 21, Sea Kings and Wessex helicopters from Squadrons 845, 846 and 848 moved stores and ammunition directly to the firing line. During the thick of the fighting, the Sea Kings from Squadron Number 826 provided antisubmarine and antisurface support offshore while Wasp and Lynx helicopters patrolled the areas along the bay and inlets. Two Gazelle gunships were shot down by Argentine ground fire while escorting Sea King helicopters on logistic missions near the front lines.

One May 25, Argentine A-4 Skyhawks attacked and sank the *Coventry* and the *Broadsword*. Working as a team with several Harriers, which provided overhead patrol cover, Sea King and Wessex helicopters from the beach conducted hasty rescue operations, successfully retrieving more than 280 survivors. During these rescue efforts, the Argentines launched another air attack against the carrier group, sinking the *Atlantic Conveyor* with a surface-skimming Exocet missile. Sea Kings from Squadron Number 826 successfully rescued thirteen men from the ship's deck as she sat helplessly burning.

The advance to Port Stanley, which began on May 28, was assisted by logistic support provided by assault helicopters. These included light Scouts, which were used to transport ammunition to and casualties from forward advancing positions. The light Gazelle helicopters, used primarily for training, never had the opportunity to fire their weapons; but they did conduct routine liaison and light logistics to front line positions.

As the war was drawing to a close in early June, assault Sea Kings from Squadron Number 825 and Wessex helicopters from Number 847 arrived at Port San Carlos aboard the *Engladine* and the *Atlantic Causeway*. They were soon joined by Squadron Number 826's detachment from Fort Austin.[3]

The final action against a surface ship in this war was against the destroyer *Glamorgan*. On June 12, she was hit in the stern by an Exocet missile. Although the missile failed to detonate, after a flight of about eighteen miles, several of the crew were killed. She was the eleventh British ship to be hit in the war.

On the final day of fighting, in the vicinity of the Tumbledown Mountains, the pilots of Squadron Number 656 flew numerous rescue missions amidst heavy gunfire. Literally flying under gunfire and grenade launchers, the Scouts and their pilots succeeded in removing the wounded to safer ground. Scouts were also presented the opportunity to fire antitank SS11 wire-guided missiles at Argentine bunkers. They achieved two direct hits—a fitting last helicopter encounter.

Fleet Air Arm helicopters provided round-the-clock ASW services throughout the war. Reports indicate, for example, that Squadron Number 820's Sea Kings alone flew 1560 hours just in May. Furthermore, approximately eighty Sea Kings and Wessex helicopters contributed to the land battle by providing transportation of troops and supplies to the scene of the action. They also provided close air support for ground troops under some of the most difficult flying conditions.

"Urgent Fury" in Grenada

In the fall of 1983 the United States became involved in a military operation on the tiny (200-square mile) island of Grenada in the southern Caribbean theater. This joint military action, code named "Operation Urgent Fury," involved extensive use of U.S. Marine Corps and Army helicopters and marked the first time that the United States' forces conducted a vertical assault from ships at sea against a hostile shore.

The initial goal of the mission was to ensure the safety of approximately one thousand U.S. citizens and students. The students were attending the St. Georges University Medical School on the island. The quick, decisive operation would have been impossible without the use of rotary-wing aircraft.

The island, located approximately one hundred miles north of Trinidad off the coast of Venezuela, is only 10 miles by 20 miles and has a population of approximately 110,000. It was granted independence from Great Britain in 1974 and has been under Marxist rule since March 1979 when Maurice Bishop assumed power in a bloodless coup d'etat. After assuming power, Bishop turned to Cuba for help in creating the People's Revolutionary Army (PRA), with 2000 members, and the People's Revolutionary Militia with some 8000 members. At the time of the 1983 U.S. invasion, a 9000-foot airstrip at Port Salines was being constructed under the supervision of a British company with mostly Cuban labor.[4]

In June 1983, Bishop traveled to Washington in an attempt to improve relations with the United States. His deputy, Bernard Coard, and his military head, General Austin Hudson, apparently did not agree with these initiatives. On October 13, they placed Bishop under house arrest. On October 21, Bishop was assassinated by his own troops under the command of General Hudson. The United States interpreted this as a Cuban-inspired action.

While these events were taking place, the members of the Twenty-Second Marine Amphibious Unit (MAU) were preparing for what they thought would be a routine Mediterranean deployment. Marine Medium Helicopter Squadron (HMM) 261 embarked on the USS *Guam* at the Naval Station in Norfolk, Virginia on October 17, 1983 as the aviation combat element of the Twenty-Second MAU. The ship got underway on October 18 and set a course to crossdeck in the eastern Mediterranean with units from off the coast of Beirut. The entire task group consisted of twelve ships, (including the carrier *Independence*, the USS *Guam* and four other amphibious ships of the Twenty-Second MAU), two landing ship tanks (LSTs), a landing ship dock (LSD) and an landing platform dock (LPD).

Three days out of Norfolk, they received a message from the Joint

Chiefs of Staff directing them to turn due south. At that point all they knew was to prepare for "neo-ops" in a hostile environment on the island of Grenada.[5] There was little information available at the time and it would be a few days before they would receive reliable intelligence. The only detailed information on the area available aboard the *Guam* consisted of a few *National Geographic* magazines and some standard non-tactical world maps.

"Urgent Fury" involved the Eighty-Second Airborne Division with fixed-wing aircraft and Sikorsky-built UH-60A Black Hawk helicopters, as well as the UH-1N, AH-1 TOW, CH-53D and CH-46F helicopters assigned to the Twenty-Second MAU. This was the first use of the UH-60A Black Hawk in combat assault, medical evacuation and transport roles.

When the group arrived in the vicinity of Grenada on October 23,* Vice Admiral Joseph Metcaff III's battle staff was sent to the *Guam*. They brought the detailed maps necessary for conducting the assault. These included a contingency support package containing virtually everything the helicopter crews would need to know such as possible beach sites and landing zones (LZs) on the island. For the first time the members of HMM-261, under the command of Lieutenant Colonel Granville Amos, knew what they might face when they began flight operations.

The operation was set to begin at 5:30 A.M. on October 25. The mission was to conduct an invasion of the island along with the U.S. Army's Eighty-Second Airborne Division.

On the eastern side of the island, four hundred Marines of the Twenty-Second MAU were to conduct a combined surface and heliborne assault on Pearls Airfield just before daybreak on October 25. The U.S. Army's Eighty-Second Airborne was to jump into the airfield at Port Salines on the southeastern tip, which was where most of the students were believed to be located.[6]

On D-day, the operation called for the troop-laden helicopters of HMM-261 to secure the Pearls Airfield, conduct a surface assault across the beach near the approach end of the runway and drop in a reserve company at a site located somewhat to the south of Pearls. However, a SEAL (Sea, Air and Land) team dropped into the area the night before to survey the land reported that the beach grading was not acceptable for a surface assault, so it was decided to go in only with the heliborne assault.

A 250-foot hill located near the perimeter of the airstrip at Pearls Airfield drew the attention of the battle staff aboard the *Guam*. Intelligence reports told of possible antiaircraft artillery (AAA) sites on the hill. The AAA's were M52 Russian-made ZSU-23 12.7 mm quad-barrel machine guns—highly effective antiaircraft weapons. So, instead of opting to roll into the airfield, Lieutenant Colonel Amos chose another site called "LZ Race Track," approximately seven hundred meters to the south of the airfield.

*Incidentally, this coincided with the terrorist bombing of the Marine Barracks in Beirut.

The pilots of HMM-261 lifted the first helicopter at 3:15 A.M. on Tuesday morning, October 25, in the middle of a blinding thunderstorm. Fortunately, the storm soon cleared, and they got twenty-two aircraft airborne for a 5:30 A.M. "L-Hour": twelve CH-46s, four CH-53D's, four AH-1 TOW Cobra gunships and two UH-1N Hueys. They headed inland in the "turf mode," meaning they hugged the terrain in order to mask their approach. Not long after that, the 550 members of the Seventy-Fifth Ranger Group were para-dropped on Point Salines Airfield from C-130E Hercules cargo planes of the 317th Tactical Air Wing (TAW). The Rangers encountered strong resistance from two well-armed Cuban Army light infantry battalions and some six hundred armed Cuban construction workers[7] in tactically advantageous positions. The AC-130s were called in to deal with the defenders.

Still, the fighting at Pearls was light. The HMM-261 helicopters ended up using landing zone "Buzzard," near the race track, which was covered with forty- to sixty-foot palm trees. They managed to get their helicopters down by putting them in divisions of four at about one- to two-minute intervals. Fortunately, the assault company experienced very little small arms fire at this landing zone.

As for the AAA piece on the hill overlooking Pearls airfield, the troops manning it squeezed off a couple of bursts, but laid down their arms after the AH-1 TOW Cobras made an appearance.

By 10:00 A.M. on D-Day, both Pearls Airport and the Port Salines Airfields near St. Georges were considered secure. St. Georges was then prepared for the arrival of the Eighty-Second Airborne Division flown in from Fort Bragg by fixed-wing C-141 Starlifters.

Once HMM-261 had the assault company established at Pearls, the helicopters returned to the ships waiting offshore and picked up the reserve company, which was then dropped in the little town of Grenville, a short distance south of LZ Race Track. There was virtually no resistance waiting for them at Grenville.

At approximately the same time, the Marine AH-1 TOW Cobra gunships, which had worked with the Marine assault company at Pearls, were turned over to the commander of the task force on Grenada. This was the commanding general of the Eighty-Second Airborne. These gunships worked armed reconnaissance and support with Army units that were trying to break out of the Port Salines area. Two Cobras were shot down and three crew members were killed.

These two HMM-261 Cobras took heavy ground fire, and one of them was hit with exploding machine gun bullets, forcing it to make a crash landing in the center of the soccer field at St. Georges. Even though the pilot, Captain Timothy B. Howard, USMC, was badly wounded* he managed to land upright. The copilot gunner, Captain Jeb Seagle, was knocked unconscious by the initial rounds that hit the aircraft. He regained consciousness when the aircraft came to rest. He managed to

*Captain Howard brought his stricken AH-1S Cobra gunship safely to the ground in spite of multiple fractures of his right leg, a severed upper right arm and shrapnel wounds in his neck.

grab Captain Howard, who had fallen out of the cockpit, by his shirt collar and dragged him to safety—approximately fifty meters away from the burning wreckage. In his efforts to evade and draw the attention of some approaching members of the People's Revolutionary Army, he was cut down approximately 100 meters away from the crash site.

The pilot that crashed in the soccer field was the wingman, flying behind and outside the leader. The lead aircraft of the section was flown by Major Pat Jiguere and his copilot, Captain Jeffrey Scharver. Upon identifying the crash site, they sent out a May-Day, a call for help. Major Mel DeMars, who was airborne at the time in a CH-46, responded to the call and proceeded to the crash site with Captain Jiguere providing suppressive fire. The CH-46 landed near the burning Cobra. Gunnery Sergeant Kelly Neighte, who was the gunner aboard the aircraft, vaulted from the helicopter and managed to get Captain Howard on board. The CH-46 remained on the ground for four to five minutes, searching for signs of Captain Seagle. With no sight of Captain Seagle and the Cobra running out of ammunition, they were forced at that point to leave the scene.

English-speaking witnesses, who were interviewed later, said Seagle was shot about 100 meters on the beach side of the crash site. He was picked up and paraded through the city the following night. His body was handed over to the Marines on shore the following day by a funeral parlor director.[8]

While escaping, Major Jiguere's Cobra, which was out of ammunition, made "dummy runs" on antiaircraft sites to draw fire away from the CH-46, which had more men aboard. As a result, his Cobra was shot down and crashed off a nearby peninsula, killing him and Captain Scharver.*

Meanwhile, the Army was still building up their strength in the vicinity of St. Georges, and there wasn't much activity at Pearls Airstrip. The decision was made to move the Marine reserve company out of Grenville to the western side of the island. From there they could move south to Port Salines and link up with the Army.

And so mid-afternoon of D-Day found HMM-261 looking for a suitable landing zone on the other side of the island. Their first inclination was to use another race course, this one just north of the city of St. Georges, called Queen's Park Race Course. Lieutenant Colonel Amos made an outstanding decision when he elected not to use the race course because of all the AAA installations that had been found in and around the city of St. Georges and Pearls Airfield. Rather, they went a little further north to where there was beach road that runs along the entire western perimeter of the island. The Huey with the Marine Aviation Unit Air Liaison Officer (MAU ALO) and the battalion commander on board went a little further north to a point called Grand Mal Beach. This location offered some landing sites, although not ideal, which could be used to move in the foot soldiers of the Golf Company. The battalion commander

---

*Account by Captain Timothy B. Howard, USMC

and the MAU commander decided to make the move late in the afternoon on D-Day, which they did by using surface assault.

Helicopter transports moved the reserve company out of Grenville to Grand Mal during the hours of darkness to protect the aircraft from any AAA threat. This means everything was flown back into Pearls late that Sunday afternoon, and about 2:15 A.M. the next morning (D+1) they started cycling sections of two out of Pearls back into Grenville. From Grenville they took the reserve company to the southwestern side of the island counterclockwise and started rolling into "LZ Fuels," which was the Grand Mal LZ. It was called "Fuels" because there were fuel storage tanks located there. The helicopters were brought in a single ship at a time by using one of the Huey's equipped with night vision goggles as a pathfinder. The last of the CH-53D's made its final drop just as the sun was coming up. The mission was uneventful; no small arms fire was reported.

The Marine battalion found a mint-condition ZSU-23-2 AAA machine-gun and a 75 mm Chinese recoilless rifle at LZ Racetrack. It was clear that had the invasion not been a total surprise, the situation could have been significantly worse for HMM-261. By that time, mid-day D+1, what resistance there was began to dissipate rapidly and the PRA began to disband.

At that point, the Marines thought they were going to have a chance to get some rest. However, at about 1:00 P.M. they received word from the flag bridge of the battle staff to launch all of the transports into Port Salines Airfield to await further instructions from the commanding general of the U.S. Ground Forces in Grenada. Lieutenant Colonel Amos was the first to launch in a Huey. All the CH-46E's and CH-53D's flew into Port Salines. There they received a mission brief which called for rescuing a large group of students holed up in a building at the Grand Anse Beach campus.

When the Eighty-Second Airborne dropped into "True Blue Campus" at Port Salines they found approximately 350 students, but there was a large group of students at another location. Fortunately, an ex-Army Ranger was a student in the other group trapped on the Grand Anse Beach campus. He had managed to establish telephone contact with the division headquarters, which was in the terminal area of Port Salines Airport. He said he had approximately three hundred students, dependents and selected nationals barricaded in a two-story dormitory on the beach.

HMM-261 took with them the Second Battalion of the Seventy-Fifth Rangers under the command of Colonel Ralph Hackler. Lieutenant Colonel Amos and Colonel Hackler, as the helicopter airborne coordinator, were in the command and control Huey with radio packs and a radio operator. Fire support was provided by a section of A-7 and HC-130 gunships.

Initially, H-Hour was set for 3:00 P.M., but due to a late call from the students asking for a delay because two people were still trying to scramble to the dormitory, the H-Hour was moved to 4:15 P.M. The flight took off from Port Salines with nine CH-46s and four CH-53D's. The pilots masked the flight by using the terrain as much as they could. The two Cobras that were left provided close-in fire support, but one of them went down because of a hydraulics problem.

The A-7s were worked; Lieutenant Colonel Amos brought them in for runs on a couple of sites at a hill mass just inland. The Rangers covering force was brought in with the first nine aircraft. The plan was for the CH-53D division lead to actually extract the students. This was done under sporadic mortar fire on the beach. The count was 329 students, selected U.S. nationals and dependents.

The beach area was very narrow with a grade. One of the CH-46s was damaged by ground fire, went down and was eventually scrapped. The birds bobbled two thirds in the water as the students were extracted. The last two CH-46s were used to get the Rangers out, and they effected a linkup with the Army at a place called the Ross Point Hotel.

This marked the end of the first forty-eight hours of the operation. HMM-261 had flown 306 hours cyclic operations off of the *Guam*'s deck with the same pilots, the same deck crew and the same air boss.

On October 27, the main assault on the town of St. Georges on the southwestern part of the island began with Marine helicopter landings supported by A-6, A-7E and AC-130H aircraft. During this engagement, a number of Rangers were killed or injured and three Eighty-Second Aviation Battalion UH-60A Black Hawk helicopters, which had flown in from a staging area in the Barbados some 200 miles away, crashed while landing troops at a suspected stronghold on the town's outskirts. The last significant resistance was at Fort Rupert. Fort Rupert was eventually taken, but not without the loss of three helicopters: two AH-1 TOW's and one CH-46.[9]

On May 1, after Grenada had calmed down, a small amphibious assault was conducted on the island of Carriacou, just to the north, where some of the PRA were allegedly hiding. The excursion to Carriacou was uneventful except for the discovery of a cache of arms. The whole operation only took about half a day.

Mopping up operations continued for at least two weeks, with AH-1s active until well into November.[10] By that time, many of the units on Grenada had been ordered to Beirut.

United States casualties amounted to 18 killed and 116 wounded. The Grenadian casualty figures were 45 killed and 337 wounded. Of the Grenadians dead, 24 were civilians, including 21 killed in an accidental bombing. Among the some 800 Cubans on the island, 24 were killed and an additional 59 wounded in action. None of the United States civilians were killed or injured.

Combat Missions: The 1990s and Beyond

Rotary-wing aircraft have become indispensable on the battlefield. Now that it's been realized that their costs are worth the benefits, no military tactician or operations planner with helicopters available would fail to use them. More than four decades of experience has proven that vertical lift aircraft are far more versatile in combat than other aircraft. As they evolved from autogiros into true helicopters, technology solved the problems limiting their capabilities. Technology has given the helicopter ever increasing efficiency, reliability, maintainability and survivability on the battlefield and at sea. And as their capabilities have expanded, so have their missions.

The aerodynamics of the rotor system was the first major problem to overcome. The fabrication of the fully articulated* and the "teetering" two-bladed rotor head designs** were the first major steps that allowed helicopters to be controllable in flight with minimum vibrations.

The next major problem was power. During the 1940s and 1950s, helicopters were underpowered because they had to rely on bulky, heavy, inefficient reciprocating piston engines. These had very poor horsepower-to-weight and maintenance-to-flight hour ratios which resulted in poor performance, inefficient operations, low reliability, poor lifting capacity and short range.

For the early pilots, ingenuity was often the only means available to deal with such shortcomings and complete the mission at hand. Often, when the weather was hot and the loads heavy, they had to "milk" their noisy, vibrating aircraft off the ground. This meant taking advantage of extra performance achieved by using the free extra lift in forward flight called "translational lift." This phenomenon allows a helicopter to maintain forward flight at less power than it takes to maintain a hover.

The advent of the gas turbine engine with its enormous power, more favorable horsepower-to-weight ratio, greater efficiency and impressive reliability was the single most important breakthrough in helicopter technology. From the early 1960s, this new power plant expanded helicopter missions significantly. Missions previously not possible were destined to become reality; helicopters could be just as effective at combat offensive operations as they were in supporting roles.

So it seems that technology has solved the major aerodynamic prob-

---

*The "fully articulated" rotor system hub design allows the rotor blades to flap up and down and lead and lag while rotating during forward flight. This reduces vibration and increases control. It is used in the SH-3 Sea King, the CH-46 Sea Knight and the CH-53 Sea Stallion.

**This is a relatively simple rotor head design that allows the rotor blades to flap up and down and lead and lag to minimize vibration. Because it has fewer moving parts than the fully articulated designs, it is less expensive to manufacture and maintain. However, it does not perform well in zero or negative G flight.

lems associated with the helicopter. This has forced the combat use of helicopters into areas previously unimagined, and yet helicopters still remain on the threshold of new missions.

Missile technology now promises to make the helicopter a true offensive weapons system, not just a support vehicle. With lighter, faster, longer-ranged and more accurate missile systems, the helicopter is no longer viewed as merely a vehicle for carrying sensors, troops and gravity launched weapons. To the list of missions traditionally associated with helicopters—combat logistics, battlefield reconnaissance, medical evacuation and search and rescue—missile technology promises to add missions which were previously thought to be exclusively for fixed-wing aircraft. For example, antisubmarine, light attack, antiship, antiarmor and antiaircraft (air-to-air) missions are now possible.

Antisubmarine Warfare

When Lieutenant (later Admiral) Alfred M. Pride, USN, landed the United States Navy's first autogiro, the Pitcairn XOP-1 on board the USS *Langley* on September 23, 1931 a new chapter of naval aviation was opened. The true helicopter would soon follow, and was destined for a long career.

The early Navy helicopter experiments were rather crude, but effective enough to encourage the development of systems, sensors and tactics. In 1949, the U.S. Navy's Unit VX-1 at Key West, Florida, was assigned the responsibility of developing helicopter antisubmarine warfare (ASW). In the spring of the following year, ten Sikorsky H-19s (designated the HO4S1) were procured and equipped with a new sensor known as the "dipping sonar." Until that time, VX-1 had been using HRP-1 helicopters, stripped of their fabric (in order to improve hover performance by reducing overall weight) and equipped with the AN/AQS-4 sonar. These soon gave way to the Piasecki HUP as the interim ASW helicopter until the arrival of the H-19s.

The Navy's first dedicated ASW helicopter squadron was Helicopter Antisubmarine Squadron (HS) One established at the Naval Air Station at Key West alongside VX-1. The establishment of three more such squadrons followed in 1952.

The next Navy helicopter to be widely used for ASW was the Sikorsky HSS-1 (later the H-34) which also came equipped with a dipping sonar. It was so successful it became accepted as the standard helicopter for the ASW mission until the SH-3 Sea King arrived on the scene. It was the first U.S. Navy helicopter designed and built, with gas turbine engines, specifically for the ASW mission. First ordered in December 1957, the SH-3s are still serving today.[1] Clearly the most successful helicopter ever to serve in the fleet, it is being flown in nearly fifty percent of the U.S. Navy's helicopter squadrons.

But employing the use of helicopters aboard hunter-killer carriers for antisubmarine warfare did not stop with the SH-3. The destroyers and fast frigates which are assigned to the carriers are an effective part of the ASW team, and it was soon discovered that helicopters could be used to enhance their capabilities as well. This became known as "light" antisubmarine warfare because helicopters deployed with the aviation capable "small boys" have to be small and light. A relatively new innovation, the Kaman SH-2D Sea Spite, which was small, yet powerful enough to carry out this mission, became the airborne part of a great system integrating the helicopter with ships' weapons. It became known as the Light Airborne Multipurpose System (LAMPS) Mk I. On July 31, 1973 Helicopter Antisubmarine Squadron (HSL) Thirty-Three became the U.S. Navy's first LAMPS Mk I squadron which provided helicopter support of small ASW Navy ships. This was the first time in U.S. Naval Aviation that ships' weapons systems were integrated with those of an aircraft. This greatly extended the sensor range and the accuracy of the weapons systems far over the horizon. It also increased the ships' ability to attack quickly.

As of 1985, 60 percent of all U.S. Navy ships were helicopter capable. There are currently six HSL squadrons in the U.S. Navy.

The future holds great promise for the LAMPS concept. The LAMPS Mk III program got underway with the introduction of the new Sikorsky state-of-the-art SH-60B Seahawk helicopter at HSL-42 in October 1984 at the Naval Air Facility in Mayport, Florida. A derivative of the U.S. Army's UH-60A Black Hawk, full-scale development of the SH-60B began in February 1978. It is an ASW avionics wonder with surface search radar, magnetic anomaly detection (MAD) equipment, an acoustic processor and sophisticated communication links with the ship. The ship has four LAMPS stations, three of them in the combat information center.* The fourth is the acoustic sensor in the ship's sonar spaces. The SH-60B is also capable of carrying depth bombs and homing torpedoes. (MAD) equipment, an acoustic processor and sophisticated communication links with the ship. The ship has four LAMPS stations, three of them in the combat information center.* The fourth is the acoustic sensor in the ship's sonar spaces. The SH-60B is also capable of carrying depth bombs and homing torpedoes.

In the spring of 1984, a $50.9 million contract with Sikorsky Aircraft was signed for full-scale development and production options for a Seahawk variant to be designated the SH-60F. These will replace the aging SH-3 Sea Kings on board carriers. The "CV-Helo" Seahawk will be equipped with a dipping sonar but without the sonobouy launcher, cargo hook, radar, electron support, MAD and data link systems. It is officially tasked with "CV Inner Zone ASW" which means that it will detect and destroy hostile submarines close to the carrier battle group. The U.S. Navy anticipates a need for as many as 175 CV-Helos.

---

*The three LAMPS stations in the ship's combat information center are: air tactical control, remote radar and electronic warfare support. The LAMPS crew aboard the ship have remote control via data link of acoustic, radar and electronic warfare functions on the SH-60B.

Antiship

The Falkland Islands War demonstrated the devastating power of state of the art weapons, especially the anti-ship missiles such as the French-made Exocet surface-skimming missile which slammed into and sank several British warships. Air-to-surface missile experiments in the U.S. Navy were seen as early as 1972 when a Kaman UH-2C Sea Sprite helicopter test fired an AIM-7 Sparrow (built by Raytheon) against surface targets. These experiments were conducted at the Naval Air Test Center, Pacific Missile Range at Point Mugu, California. The Sparrow was being considered for use in the LAMPS Mk I helicopters.[2]

U.S. Navy studied the need for helicopter antiship missiles as early as 1979. The idea was resurrected in 1982, shortly after the Falklands War. Most recently, the Navy approved of the FFG's (Fast Frigate Guided Missiles) SH-60B LAMPS Mk IIIs being equipped with the newest versions of the Norwegian-built Penguin Mk2 Mod 7 missile. A fire-and-forget, antiship weapon, it is designed to allow the helicopter to fire at its target and immediately break off to avoid counterattack. The missile proceeds toward its target, after being fed trajectory instructions, using its own navigation system. Then, when it's in close, it switches to its infrared sensor to aim directly for the ship's waterline. This impressive weapon will likely see fleet introduction in the early 1990s.

The French Aérospatiale AS 332F1 Super Puma helicopter can carry two AM 39 Exocet air-to-surface missiles.

Antiarmor

There are many who believe that rotary-wing aircraft have far greater potential on the battlefield than has thus far been utilized, particularly in the area of antiarmor missions. One Soviet faction maintains that the tank is being rendered obsolete by the helicopter and improved antiarmor munitions. That contention will be reinforced with the introduction of the fire-and-forget antitank missile which will put the tank at a further disadvantage.[3]

The combat helicopter is a "force multiplier" in both land and sea battles. Helicopter units such as AH-1S platoons or AH-64 tank killer teams can deliver a greater concentration of antitank fire from concealed positions than any ground system. Furthermore, the mobility and flexibility of the helicopter provides a greater capability to concentrate this firepower wherever needed.[4]

The Hughes-built AH-64 Apache attack helicopter is a classic example of the integration of antiarmor missiles and the rotary-wing vehicle. Equipped with sixteen Hellfire laser-guided antiarmor missiles and the remarkable Target Acquisition and Designation Sight (TADS) and Pilot Night Vision Sensor (PNVS) systems, it can strike targets quickly and accurately day or night. The Hellfire missile is also being integrated with the Bell-built U.S. Marine Corps' AH-1T+ Super Cobra gunship.

Helicopter antiarmor capabilities are only beginning to be explored. France and West Germany are currently jointly developing an antitank helicopter to serve their anticipated needs. The German version is known as the PAH2* while the French variant is designated the HAC5G.** With a gross weight of 10,570 pounds, this single-rotor gunship will be equipped with as many as eight HOT 2 or ATGW 3 antitank missiles and four Stinger antiaircraft missiles. It will also be configured with nose-mounted television cameras, forward-looking infrared sensors and laser range finders.

Helicopter Airborne Mine Countermeasures

There is another helicopter mission which is not offensive in nature. It is a very interesting task which cannot be carried out by any other type of aircraft—airborne mine countermeasures. This mission applies the inherent mobility and quick response of the helicopter to the vital mission of getting battle groups safely away from mines.

As early as 1950, helicopters were used for mine countermeasures (MCM) in Korea. At that time, their MCM capability was limited to mine hunting. Some three thousand North Korean mines in Wonsan Harbor delayed operations for more than a week and sank two minesweeping ships. Experiments during the following two decades led to the use of the Sikorsky-built RH-3 and the RH-53D helicopters.

Over the years, as the Russian mine threat became apparent, the Navy created a mine countermeasures detachment in Helicopter Combat Support Squadron (HC) Six with thirteen modified CH-53A Sea Stallions. This detachment became the Navy's first bonafide minesweeping squadron on April 1, 1971 and was designated Helicopter Mine Countermeasures Squadron (HM) Twelve. The CH-53A's were eventually replaced with sixteen RH-53D Sikorsky helicopters which were designed specifically for the MCM mission. Able to tow a variety of mechanical, acoustic and influence minesweeping devices, the squadron proved very effective during "Operation End Sweep" in Haiphong Harbor in 1973, and "Operation Nimbus Stream" and "Operation Star" in the Suez Canal in 1974 and 1975.

From HM-12, two other airborne mine countermeasures (AMCM) squadrons were formed, HM-14 and HM-16. HM-12, at the Naval Air Station in Norfolk, Virginia, conducts fleet readiness training. HM-14 and HM-16 participate in world-wide AMCM support.

A typical example of the AMCM community's fast response and flexibility was seen during the period from August to October 1984 when Helicopter Mine Countermeasures Squadron Fourteen (HM-14), under the command of Commander Chester F. Harrison, USN, was involved in "Operation Intense Look." The deployment of the squadron in response

*PAH2 stands for Panzerabwehrhubschrauber 2nd Generation.

**HAC3F stands for Hélicoptère anti-char avec missile anti-char de 3ème génération.

to the mining of the Gulf of Suez and the possible mining of Saudi Arabian Red Sea Ports presented several unique challenges and opportunities.

As reported by the Navy, on August 3 the squadron received orders from the Joint Chiefs of Staff to begin tearing down six RH-53D helicopters in anticipation of deployment in response to mining in the Gulf of Suez. All six aircraft were torn down and ready within twenty-four hours for shipment. On August 6, two hundred squadron personnel were deployed along with four helicopters from Norfolk to Rota, Spain in answer to the assistance request from the government of Egypt. In Rota, the squadron's equipment and the four helicopters were reassembled and loaded on the USS *Shreveport.* Within seventy-four hours after leaving Norfolk, all aircraft were fully operational and the squadron was ready to begin minehunting. Following a transit of the Mediterranean Sea and Suez Canal, the squadron arrived in the Gulf of Suez on August 17, 1984. Actual mine hunting operations began at dawn the next day in the vicinity of Ras Shukayr.

The cornerstone of the airborne mine countermeasures (AMCM) effort in the Gulf of Suez was heavy reliance on a new mine hunting sonar, the AQS-14. Only recently introduced to the operational fleet, initial training with this new equipment began only a month and a half prior to the deployment. From the beginning of "Operation Intense Look," personnel, aircraft and equipment successfully worked together to complete the task on schedule, conducting dawn-to-dusk flight operations for twenty-two consecutive days in search of mines. Operating in conjunction with the USNS *Harkness,** the squadron searched approximately 200 square miles, accumulating 161 tow hours with the AQS-14. A total of forty-four contacts were located; thirty-two of these were reacquired by sonar and reevaluated as nonmine-like, eight were investigated by divers and the remaining four were investigated by remote controlled vehicle. These turned out to be 50-gallon barrels, pieces of pipe, coral heads and other trash.

On August 12, 1984, the remaining ten squadron personnel and three helicopters were deployed from Norfolk to Jeddah, Saudi Arabia to meet the mine threat in the Red Sea. Within forty hours of arrival, HM-14 Detachment One began operations in the approaches and the main channels to the port of Jeddah using magnetic and acoustic minesweeping devices. The detachment embarked on the USS *Lasalle* on August 20 and conducted minesweeping operations near the ports of Yanbu and Gixan, Saudi Arabia. Additionally, minesweeping operations were conducted at the southern end of the Red Sea in the Strait of Bab al Mandeb. The USS *America* carrier battle group was led through the strait by the HM-14 Detachment One helicopters and the USS *Lasalle.* A total of seventy-seven tow hours were accumulated by the detachment. Operations in Saudi Arabia concluded in late September. The detachment redeployed to Norfolk in early October.[5]

*A military sealift command hydrographic survey ship operated for the Naval Oceanographic Office. It was equipped with a commercial side-looking sonar which served well in the mine hunting role.

On September 17, 1984, the main body of HM-14 was released from operations in the Gulf of Suez and started back to Rota, Spain. Three days later, the squadron was diverted and ordered to stand by off the coast of Beirut, Lebanon in order to provide the support required by the American Embassy there following the bombing incident of September 20. In addition, the squadron flew medevac and other logistic flights. On October 5, HM-14 again began its transit back to Rota for disassembly of aircraft and equipment and subsequent C-5 airlift to Norfolk. The squadron maintained a mission capable rate of greater than 85 percent over the two month period. The detachment working with the government of Saudi Arabia maintained a mission capable rate of 82 percent during their operations.[6]

While the United States may have the largest and most sophisticated airborne mine countermeasures assets, it is not the only major maritime power to have the capability. The Soviet Union has used Mil Mi-8 Hip and Mi-14 Haze-B helicopters for this mission. Mi-14s were allegedly deployed to the Red Sea aboard the *Leningrad* as part of an international minesweeping operation. Japan also performs airborne mine countermeasures using specially configured CH-46 tandem-rotor helicopters.

Aerial Combat

Helicopters have become more threatening because of their increasing survivability and firepower. Traditionally, only troops on the ground needed to fear helicopter gunships. But now, aircraft of all types need to be wary of helicopters.

Air-to-ground rockets have been used effectively from helicopters for many years in combat against ground enemy positions. Now, antiarmor missiles such as Hellfire are making rotary-wing aircraft even more threatening.

In the modern battlefield scenario, both sides will employ heavily armed helicopters. Now the enemies of combat helicopters are also airborne and the threat must be countered. If tanks are the best weapon against tanks, than it follows that the best way of dealing with armed helicopters is with armed helicopters.[7] So helicopters will be pitted against each other in a way that was once thought to be only a fixed-wing evolution—air-to-air combat.

With the advent of light-weight, heat-seeking air-to-air missiles, helicopters* are equipped to engage in one-on-one evasive maneuvering, popularly known as "dog fighting."[8] There is evidence that helicopter-against-helicopter combat engagements have already taken place in the war between Iran and Iraq. On April 24, 1981 the Iranian News Agency reported that during air-to-air combat Iranian helicopters "blew up two enemy attack helicopters during a dogfight." There was no confirmation of this or mention of the types of helicopters or missiles used. In September 1983, another such event took place near the Basra front that

*At the present time there are four air defense missiles used by the U.S. Marine Corps and the U.S. Army: the IR homer AIM-9L and the Stinger, the laser homer Hellfire and the laser beam riding Saber.

resulted in the downing of an Iranian AH-1J SeaCobra by an Iraqi Soviet-supplied Mi-24 Hind D. The British Aviation Research Group maintains that this incident was the world's first air-to-air combat between helicopters.[9]

It can be assumed that the major combat helicopters of the Western world, such as the United States' AH-1T Super Cobra and the AH-64 Apache, the German PAH-2, the French SA 342 Gazelle and the British WG 13 Lynx, will not be immune to aerial attack from rotary-wing battlefield aircraft. The Russians were the last major power to develop dedicated attack helicopters, but they have arrived with great impact. As Soviet attack helicopters increasingly move toward antihelicopter operations, the fire-and-forget, air-to-air Stinger begins to present serious problems.[10]

To deal with these developments, the U.S. Navy (among others) has been studying helicopters in air-to-air combat evasive maneuvering. The Naval Air Test Center, Patuxent River, Maryland, began studying the problem as early as 1982 and began flight testing in the spring of 1983. Officially known as the AH-1S Helicopter Evasive Maneuvering Flight Test, this project, and those of the U.S. Army and other western nations, will lead to unique aerial tactics and the refined maneuvers necessary to quickly target the enemy's helicopters while avoiding their deadly missiles.

The Navy, Marine Corps and Army have endeavored to develop new helicopter weapons systems and to train rotary-wing aviators in evasive maneuvering.[11] The U.S. Marine Corps conducts evasive maneuvering training on a regular basis with the Marine Aviation Weapons and Tactics Squadron (MAWTS) One at the Marine Corps Air Station in Yuma, Arizona. At Yuma, the Marine rotary-wing pilots learn that evasive maneuvers are the best way for a helicopter and its crew to survive in a threatening environment. They are taught to evade ground threats and air threats, the latter including helicopters and fixed-wing aircraft. Because many nations are employing large numbers of attack helicopters with high-technology weapon systems, tactics and maneuvers could mean the difference between losing and winning.

The formula for dealing with the problem is relatively simple. Effective antihelicopter air combat requires the harmonization of four factors: the vehicle, the weapons, the crew and the environment.[12] Improving any of these improves the probability of winning. One conclusion that can be drawn from the data available is that the performance of the delivery vehicle may be subsidiary to the performance of its weapons and fire control system. This means that many countries with meager resources could acquire commercial helicopters armed with high performance weapons systems.[13] So even countries with relatively few military resources could employ helicopters with state of the art missile systems.

The Soviet Union introduced the HIND attack helicopter in 1971 and it is likely to be in their inventory at least into the 1990s. The HIND-E, armed with sophisticated missiles, guns and bombs, will be a formidable threat throughout its service life. Today, the AT-6 stands as the most prominent guided missile in the world because of its range and speed. But more importantly, the AT-6 can be used in an antihelicopter air-to-air role. Hind-E's have carried AT-6s on the inboard pylons as well as in the standard mounting locations on the outboard winglets.

A major joint initiative by the Army and the Air Force was begun in 1978. Called "Joint Countering of Attack Helicopters," or "J-CATCH," it has resulted in simulations and tests. There has been a proliferation of studies, proposals, papers and tests all aimed at meeting the HIND threat. J-CATCH is perhaps the most impressive in scope and detail.[14]

A new Russian attack helicopter under development, code named Mi-28 Havoc, is a strong indication that the combat helicopter is destined to play a greater role in the land battle. The Mi-28, which bears a striking resemblance to the AH-64 in both size and performance, will serve primarily in the antiarmor role. There are indications that it will be equipped with 23 mm cannons, and AT-6 antitank and SA-14 air-to-air missiles. All this indicates that the traditional military concepts of air-to-air warfare will have to be reexamined as new rotary-wing systems are brought into the combat scenario.

Combat Support

The military helicopter's most familiar roles are battlefield logistics and communications. The recently developed U.S. Army UH-60A Black Hawk gives new meaning to these missions of combat support.

During its developmental stages in 1972, it was known as Utility Tactical Transport Aircraft System (UTTAS). It was developed as a replacement for the venerable but ageing Vietnam era UH-1 Huey. The first flight of the initial production UH-6A airframe was on October 17, 1978. Deliveries to the Army began the last day of that month. Sikorsky had delivered nearly half of the planned 1107 Black Hawks by March 27, 1984.

The Black Hawk began service with the U.S. Army in its combat support transport mission at Fort Campbell, Kentucky with the 101st Airborne Division. It saw its first combat use in "Operation Urgent Fury," the invasion of Grenada, in October 1983.

One of its unique capabilities is that can self-deploy across the Atlantic Ocean to the Mediterranean theater via St. Johns, Newfoundland and the Azores. To do this, it is configured with two stubby winglets on each side of the fuselage called the External Stores Support System (ESSS). These carry additional 230-gallon fuel tanks, increasing its range to 1150 nautical miles against a 10 knot head wind. The ESSS also allows the UH-60A to carry weapons such as the M-56 mine dispenser (which carries 80 mines) or Hellfire missiles.

Just as the UH-60A is adding new dimensions to helicopter combat support today, tilt-rotor technology promises to revolutionize rotary-wing combat support in the decades to come. The tilt-rotor XV-15 technology demonstration vehicle, built by Bell Helicopter Textron, first flew on May 3, 1977 under NASA and Army sponsorship. It is a rotary-wing aircraft with the ability to hover, but by tilting the rotors forward the vehicle assumes the flight speeds and handling characteristics of an airplane. Known as the V-22 Osprey, it was first designated as the Joint Services Advanced Vertical Lift Aircraft Development (JVX) Program. It was intended to replace the U.S. Marine Corps' ageing UH-46 assault transport, the U.S. Navy's HH-3A combat search and rescue, and the U.S. Air Force's HH-53A combat rescue and special operations helicopters as well as the U.S. Army's OV-10 reconnaissance and surveillance aircraft.

In August 1982, the XV-15 proved its adaptability to ship operations by making fifty-four landings on and takeoffs from the carrier USS *Tripoli.* Thus it fulfilled the amphibious vertical assault role.

The V-22 will be delivered to the U.S. Marine Corps in 1991 and to the U.S. Navy, Air Force and Army beginning in 1992.

Fourth Generation Military Helicopter

Technology promises to expand the capabilities of helicopters to the farthest limits of the laws of physics. With "high tech" knowhow, future helicopters will be built from non-metalic materials, use sophisticated aerodynamic designs in order to acheive maximum possible speeds, be equipped with infared and low light sensors and carry more types of weapons than any other flying machine. Furthermore, they will be easier to fly with digital flight controls, including microprocessors and fly-by-wire systems. In short, the limitations of helicopters will be challenged and solved with radical changes in design, aerodynamics, materials and perhaps even terminology; i.e., vertical lift vs. helicopter.

There are a few new helicopters under development. The previously mentioned West German and French antitank PAH-2 is one such example. The first prototype is expected anytime, and the first delivery to the French military could be as early as 1991. The PAH-2 would be offered in three versions. Each would use essentially the same airframe and engines, but weapons and some other systems would vary depending upon the country and the intended role. Planned primarily for the antitank mission, it will be capable of being equipped with a variety of weapons: For example, 30 mm Giat-AM 30781 turret mounted guns, four air-to-air missiles and two SNEB 68 rockets; or eight HOT antitank missiles and four air-to-air Stinger missiles; or eight ATGW 3 antitank (fire-and-forget missiles). Its sensors will include mast-mounted TV, FLIR and laser range finder. The MBB* PAH-2 main rotor will be all-composite and equipped with elastomeric bearings developed by MBB.

* Messerschmitt-Bölkow-Blohm Gmbh.

Another example is the EH-101, a joint British and Italian antisubmarine warfare helicopter.* Conceived as a replacement for the Sea King ASW helicopter, this 28,000 pound triple-engine helicopter will perform several ship-based maritime missions: antisubmarine warfare, antiship surveillance, anti-surface vessel, amphibious operations, search and rescue, airborne early warning and vertical replenishment. It is estimated that one thousand military and civilian EH-101s will be built by the year 2000.

Meanwhile the Agusta/Westland A129 Mangusta (Mongoose) antitank helicopter is under development. The first prototype flew September 15, 1983 at Cascino Costa, Italy. At the present time, there are three of the twin-engine prototypes built by Construzioni Aeronautiche G. Augusta, Italy. Designed to specifically meet Italian Army needs, it will be capable of light attack, reconnaissance and air-to-air combat. Approximately sixty will be purchased for the Italian Army through 1990, and there is a strong possibility of the British Army purchasing it for the antiarmor mission. Weighing in at only 8160 pounds, it is likely be configured with the TOW missile system.

Over the Horizon

The future capabilities of combat helicopters will be limited only by technology. The research and development presently charting the future of rotary-wing aircraft includes an impressive list of innovative ways to make helicopters do much more than they do today.

Consider these:

☐ Advancing Blade Concept (ABC), XH-59A, Sikorsky Counter Rotating blades. Its only limit on forward speed would be the Mach number of the advancing blade as it approaches the speed of sound.

☐ No Tail Rotor (NOTAR) Concept. This is a Hughes conventional helicopter with a single rotor and external propulsion system.

☐ LHX, the experimental light combat helicopter. One proposal is the Bell Advanced Tilt Rotor (BAT). This single pilot configuration aircraft is designed to expand current rotary-wing missions by incorporating features such as lift over drag 50 percent better than current helicopters, hover ceilings in excess of 10,000 feet, good high altitude performance, enhanced range with lower noise, weapons concealed until required, retractable landing gear, Vmax of 270 knots at 4000 feet/95°F, Vmax of 304 knots at 14,000 feet/standard day, and an equipped ferry mission range of 2100 nautical miles. The rotors would be 20.5 feet long.[15]

☐ X-Wing. Sikorsky, under a contract with the Defense Advance Research Projects Agency (DARPA), is developing this unique X-wing rotorcraft which is a helicopter whose rotor can be stopped in flight to form an X-shaped wing. A turboshaft/turbo fan engine would supply power in both fixed- and rotary-wing modes. It also employs the surface-

---

*EH-101 designation was originally "EHL 01" for European Helicopter Ltd. 01, but due to a secretarial error, the "l" of Ltd. was transcribed as the numeral one.

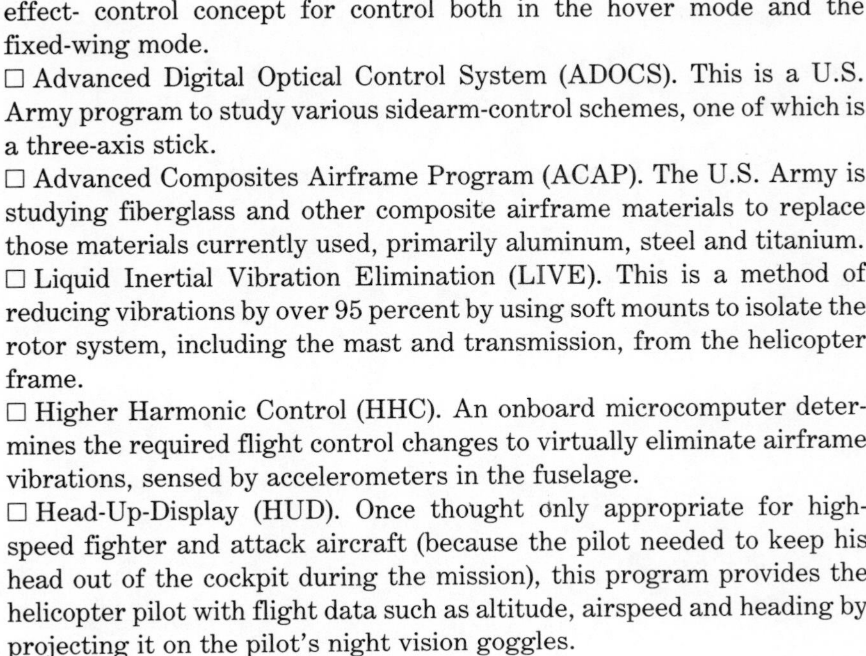

effect- control concept for control both in the hover mode and the fixed-wing mode.

☐ Advanced Digital Optical Control System (ADOCS). This is a U.S. Army program to study various sidearm-control schemes, one of which is a three-axis stick.

☐ Advanced Composites Airframe Program (ACAP). The U.S. Army is studying fiberglass and other composite airframe materials to replace those materials currently used, primarily aluminum, steel and titanium.

☐ Liquid Inertial Vibration Elimination (LIVE). This is a method of reducing vibrations by over 95 percent by using soft mounts to isolate the rotor system, including the mast and transmission, from the helicopter frame.

☐ Higher Harmonic Control (HHC). An onboard microcomputer determines the required flight control changes to virtually eliminate airframe vibrations, sensed by accelerometers in the fuselage.

☐ Head-Up-Display (HUD). Once thought only appropriate for high-speed fighter and attack aircraft (because the pilot needed to keep his head out of the cockpit during the mission), this program provides the helicopter pilot with flight data such as altitude, airspeed and heading by projecting it on the pilot's night vision goggles.

Ingenuity Made Machine

The helicopter is evidence of how man's imagination can be given physical form. Though virtually impossible only four and a half decades ago, the helicopter has developed from a fragile, under-powered novelty to a flying machine essential to modern warfare. Its versatility, capabilities and reliability have increased directly with the growth of technology. No longer is the helicopter considered a nice-to-have vehicle on the battlefield—now it is essential.

As a measure of the growing importance of rotary-wing aircraft in the United States, in 1985 the new-technology, $23 billion V-22 development program was the eighth highest priority acquisition program in the United States and the sixth most important Navy program in dollars behind the F-18, F-14, Trident missile, SSN 688 submarine and the CG-47 ship.[16]

Whether it is logistics, reconnaissance, command and control, troop transport, search and rescue, antiarmor, light attack, antiship, antisubmarine warfare, airborne mine countermeasures, antiaircraft or perhaps even electronic countermeasures, rotary-wing aircraft can do it all. That is why they are essential in modern combat.

SOURCES CONSULTED

Aircraft Year Book for 1946. New York: Lanciar Publishers, Inc., 1946.

Aircraft Year Book 1952. Washington D.C.: Lincoln Press Inc., 1952.

"Air Operations in the Malay Campaigns." *Aeroplane,* 20 April 1951, p. 470.

Allen, C. B., and Lymand, Lauren D. *The Wonderful Book on the Air.* Chicago: John C. Winston Co., 1941.

AMCM Tow Tales. Airborne Mine Countermeasures Program Division Newsletter, Naval Air Systems Command, December 1984.

"Army Policy for Aerial Fire Support and Aerial Surveillance." Study by Deputy Chief of Staff for Military Operations, U.S. Army, 29 March 1962.

Arpurt, R. J. "Aspects des opèrations heliportees en Algerie." *Foreces Aeriennes Francaises,* No. 158, (1960) pp. 637–662.

"Assault Helo Office Open (at Naval Air Systems Command)." *Naval Aviation News,* 1968, p. 3.

"Augmentation of Unit." U.S. Army Utility-Tactical Transport Helicopter Company Memorandum to Commanding General U.S. Army, Ryukyu Islands, 23 November 1962.

"Augusta A 129." *Air International* 26 (February 1984): 103–104.

Baker, W. H. "The Helicopter: Hazardous At Any Height." *U.S. Naval Institute Proceedings,* October 1970.

Bavaro, Edward J. "Soviet Helicopter Armament." *Army Aviation Digest* 30 (November 1984): 34–37.

Beaver, Paul. "US Army Aviation—Today and Tomorrow." *Armed Forces,* September 1983, pp. 346–348.

"Bell Advanced Tilt Rotor (BAT): Possible Entry to Army LHX Program." *Rotorbreeze* 33 (July/August 1984): 3.

Berger, Carl, ed. *The U.S. Air Force in Southeast Asia 1961–1973.* Washington, D.C.: Office of Air Force History, U.S. Government Printing Office, 1977.

Bethouart, Hilaire. "AVIATION: Legende L'Armée Terre." *U.S. Army Aviation Digest,* 6 (May 1960).

Bowers, Ray L. *The United States Air Force in Southeast Asia: Tactical Air Lift.* Washington, D.C.: Office of Air Force History, U.S. Government Printing Office, 1983.

Bowler, D. A. "Entente Aeronavale." *Flight Deck,* Spring 1962, pp. 15–17.

Boyne, Walter J. and Lopez, Donald S., eds. *Vertical Flight: The Age of the Helicopter.* Washington, D.C.: Smithsonian Institute Press, 1984.

Breeze, J. E. "Rotors Over The Jungle: No. 848 Naval Air Squadron in Malaya." (publication unknown), 12 March 1954, pp. 291–292.

Brewer, Frank. "HMM-261 Grenada Operations." Presentation at the Naval Helicopter Association 37th Annual Symposium, Virginia Beach, Va., 2 May 1985.

Brown, David A. "Westland Upgrading Lynx 3 Naval Roles." *Aviation Week and Space Technology,* 31 October 1983, pp. 51–52.

Caidin, Martin. *Golden Wings.* Bramhall House, 1960.

Capon, P. T. "Cierva's First Autogiros (Part 1)." *Aeroplane Monthly* 7 (April 1979): 235–240.

———. "Cierva's First Autogiros (Part 2)." *Aeroplane Monthly* 7 (May 1979): 200–205.

Chartres, John. *Helicopter Rescue.* Shepperton, England: Ian Allan Ltd., 1980.

Churchill, Winston. *The Second World War.* Boston: Houghton Mifflin Company, 1949.

Cooling, B. Franklin. "A History of U.S. Army Aviation." *Aerospace Historian* 21 (Summer/June 1974): 102–109.

Courtney, Frank T. *Flight Path: My Fifty Years of Aviation.* London: William Kimber.

de la Cierva, Don Juan. "The Autogiro." *Journal RUSI* 73 (May 1928): 304–310.

Desoutter, Denis M. *Aircraft and Missiles.* 2nd ed. New York: John De Graff Inc., 1959.

Drendel, Lou. *Gunslinger In Action.* Carrollton, Texas: Squadron/Signal Publications, Inc., 1974.

———. *Huey.* Carrollton, Texas: Squadron/Signal Publications, 1983.

"848 Naval Air Squadron." *Flight Deck,* Autumn/Winter 1960, pp. 1–44.

"848 Naval Air Squadron." *Flight Deck,* Autumn 1961, pp. 1–48.

"Eighth Transport Company (Light Helicopter) Unit History." Chronology of Units Deployed to the Republic of Vietnam. Headquarters, U.S. Army Audit Agency, 2 August 1963.

Elwell, Robert. "The Vulnerable Hind." *Air Clues,* December 1983, pp. 444–449.

Fahlstrom, Paul G. "Air-to-Air Missiles for Marine Corp and Army Helicopters." *Amphibious Warfare Review* (July 1984): 18–23.

Fazekas, James. "Sky Soldiers." *Air Power* 10 (March 1980).

Feazel, Michael. "Augusta Testing Low-Cost A129 Antitank Helicopter." *Aviation Week & Space Technology,* 10 October 1983.

———. "Europeans Expect PAH-2 Decision in July." *Aviation Week & Space Technology,* 28 May 1984.

"Fifty-seventh Transport Company (Light Helicopter) Unit History." Chronology of Units Deployed to the Republic of Vietnam. Headquarters, U.S. Army Audit Agency, 2 August 1963.

Flintham, Vic. "Invasion of Grenada." *Air Pictorial* 47 (January 1985): 8–12.

"French Airmobility." *U.S. Army Aviation Digest* 21 (March 1975): 4, 12–17.

Funkhouser, John T. "Soviet Carrier Strategy." *U.S. Naval Institute Proceedings,* December 1973, pp. 28–37.

Futrell, Robert F. *The United States Air Force in Korea 1950–1953.* Washington, D.C.: Office of Air Force History, Government Printing Office, 1981.

Gablehouse, Charles. *Helicopters and Autogiros: A History of Rotating-wing and V/STOL Aviation.* Philadelphia: J. B. Lippincott Company, 1969.

Gillies, J. D. "Weir and Cierva." *Air-Britain Digest,* April 1973, pp. 61–63.

Goodson, Betty J. "Victory in Air-to-Air Combat, The Marine Corps Way." *U.S. Army Aviation Digest* 28 (July 1982): 2–7.

Grayson, E. H., Jr. "Army Aviation 1984 to 2015." *Army Aviation Digest* 30 (November 1984): 2–7.

Gregory, H. F. *The Helicopter or Anything A Horse Can Do.* London: George Allen and Unwin Limited, 1948.

"Grenada Gamble." *Aviation Week & Space Technology,* 31 October 1983, p. 17.

Gunston, Bill. *Helicopters of the World.* Feltham, England: Temple Press Aerospace, 1983.

Harrison, Donald F. "Developments In Airmobility." *United States Army Aviation Digest* 15 (June 1969): 20–24.

Harvey, Bruce E. "Casualty Evacuation by Helicopter in Malaya." *British Medical Journal,* No. 4730 (1951), pp. 542–544.

Hasskarl, Robert A., Jr. "Early Military Use of Rotary-Wing Aircraft." *Airpower Historian* 12 (July 1965): 75–77.

"Helicopter Squadron Two (HU-2), Squadron Historical Reports." United States Naval Air Station, Lakehurst, NJ: 1 October 1948–31 December 1948; 1 July 1950–31 December 1950; 1 January 1951–30 June 1951; 1 July 1951–31 December 1951; 1 July 1952–31 December 1952; 1 January 1952–30 June 1952.

"Henrich Focke's Singular Kite, Part II." *Air International* 26 (June 1984): 291–299.

Heslin, John G. "The Air-Land Battle: A Winning Combination." *U.S. Army Aviation Digest* 30 (January 1984): 38–41.

Hezlet, Arthur. *Aircraft and Sea Power.* London: Peter Davies, 1970.

Hilbert, Marquis D. and Murray, Everett. "Use of Army Aviation in Counterinsurgency Operations." *United States Army Aviation Digest* 8 (October 1962): 3–9.

Hoyt, Edwin P. and Zaffo, George F. *Whirlybirds.* New York: Doubleday and Co., 1961.

Hubler, Richard B. *Straight Up, The Story of Vertical Flight.* New York: Duell, Sloan and Pearce.

Huertas, Salvator Mafe. "FAMET—The Spanish Army Airmobile Forces." *Aviation Week,* 27 January 1984, pp. 766–769.

Jackson, Paul. "Super Puma." *Air International* 26 (January 1984): 7–12, 33–35.

Jane's All the World's Aircraft. New York: MacMillan Company.

Johnson, Brian. *Fly Navy: The History of Maritime Aviation.* London: David & Chambers.

Karig, Walter; Cagle, Malcolm W.; and Manson, Frank A. *Battle Report: The War in Korea.* New York: Rinehart and Company, Inc., 1952.

Kay, William K. "The Army Aviation Story." *United States Army Aviation Digest* 7 (June 1961): 1–7.

Keating, Bern. *Choppers: The Illustrated Story of Helicopters in Action.* Chicago: Rand McNally and Company, 1976.

Kinnucan, Paul. "Superchoppers." *High Technology* 3 (August 1983).

Klein, Ron. "Aviation Employment in the Special Purpose Operations." *U.S. Army Aviation Digest* 30 (September 1984): 2–9.

"Korea: An Air War Report." Supplement, *The Pegasus.* Hagerstown, Maryland: The Fairchild Engine and Airplane Corporation.

Laskin, Danial. "Pax River Teams Studying Copters in Aerial Combat." *Navy Times,* 11 July 1983.

Lawrence, B. P. "The Use of Autogiros in the Evacuation of Wounded." *The Military Surgeon,* December 1933, pp. 315–321.

Lind, William S. "The Grenada Operation." Report to the Congressional Military Reform Caucus, Military Reform Institute, 5 April 1984.

McCoy, James M. "Mine Countermeasures: Who's Fooling Whom?" *United States Naval Institute Proceedings* 101 (July 1965): 40–43.

Maxwell, Alfred R. "Use of Helicopters for Rescue by the Army Air Forces." Memorandum, Requirements Division, U.S. Army, 26 February 1946.

Mersky, Peter B. and Polmar, Norman. *The Naval Air War in Vietnam.* Baltimore: The Nautical and Aviation Publishing Company of America, 1981.

Mersky, Peter B. *U.S. Marine Corps Aviation, 1912 to the Present.* Baltimore: The Nautical and Aviation Publishing Company of America, 1983.

Mesko, Jim. "Airmobile: The Helicopter War In Vietnam." Carrollton, Texas: Squadron Signal Publications, Inc., 1984.

Montross, Lynn and Prouty, Ray. "U.S. Marine Corps Helicopter Experience." *Vertiflight,* No. 4 (1984), pp. 77–80.

"Movement Directive." U.S. Army Headquarters, Ryukyu Islands Memorandum to Commanding Officer, U.S. Army Utility Tactical Transport Helicopter Company, 26 September 1962. U.S. Army Staff Office Report, October–December 1962.

Munson, Kenneth. *Helicopters and Other Rotorcraft Since 1907.* Great Britain: The Macmillian Company, 1968.

Navy Wings. Washington, D.C.: Bureau of Naval Personnel, U.S. Government Printing Office, 1955.

Neel, M. C. Jr. and Spurgeon, Lt. Col. "Medical Considerations in Helicopter Evacuation." *U.S. Armed Forces Medical Journal* 5 (Feb. 1954): 220–227.

Novosel, Michael J. "From Wood and Linen Kites to Metal Monsters." *United States Army Aviation Digest* 30 (June 1984).

Omlsted, Merle. "Helicopter Rescue: The Early Years." *Journal of the American Aviation Historical Society,* Summer 1976, pp. 112–117.

O'Rourke, Robert J. "Marine Air Operations in Northern Europe." *United States Naval Institute Proceedings,* November 1980, pp. 53–59.

Payne, Anthony; Sutton, Paul; and Thorndike, Tony. *Grenada: Revolution and Invasion.* New York: St. Martin's Press, 1984.

Polmar, Norman. "JVX" *U.S. Naval Institute Proceedings,* November 1983, pp. 155–157.

Polmar, Norman and Kennedy, Floyd D., Jr. *Military Helicopters of the World: Military Rotary-Wing Aircraft Since 1917.* Annapolis: Naval Institute Press, 1981.

"Position and Employment of USA/USMC Aviation Units." Letter of Instruction, Headquarters U.S. Military Assistance Command, Vietnam, Serial number 00239, 31 October 1962.

Rawlins, Eugene W. "Marines and Helicopters 1946–1962." Washington, D.C.: History and Museums Division, Headquarters Marine Corps, 1967.

Riley, David. "French Helicopter Operations in Algeria." *Marine Corps Gazette,* February 1958, pp. 21–26.

"Role of Aviation in Vietnam." Study by Acting Deputy Chief of Staff for Military Operations, U.S. Army, 4 April 1962.

Ross, Frank, Jr. *Flying Windmills: The Story of the Helicopter.* New York: Lothrop, Lee & Shepard Col, Inc.

Sheddon, Harry. "The World's Most Versatile Attack Helicopter—Marine AH -1T+ Supercobra." *Rotobreeze* 33 (January 1984).

"Sikorsky's Hawks." *Air International* 27 (July 1984), pp. 6–15, 45–46.

Simmonds, B. P. "Thirty Years of Helicopter Flying in the RAF." *Air Clues,* September 1983, pp. 347–349.

Slater, Group Captain. "Air Operations in Malaya." *Journal of the Royal United Services Institute for Defense Studies,* August 1957, pp. 378–387.

Smith, James P. "Air-to-Air Workshop." *U.S. Army Aviation Digest* 30 (May 1984): 3–7.

Smith, R. E. "Middle East Wasp." *Flight Deck,* No. 3 (1967) pp. 19–24.

Sprinkle, James D. "The Hueycobra, Its Origins." *Journal of the American Aviation Historical Society* 20 (Spring 1975): 30–35.

Stratemyer, General. Request for Helicopters. Memorandum, 18 January 1945.

Straubel, John F. *One Way Up.* Hiller Aircraft Company, Inc., 1964.

Sutcliffe, M. W. "Malayan Operations." *U.S. Army Aviation Digest* 8 (October 1962): 10–15.

Swanborough, F. G. *Vertical Flight Aircraft of the World.* United States: Aero Publishers, 1964.

Taylor, John W. R., ed. *Jane's Pocket Book of Major Combat Aircraft.* New York: MacMillan Publishing Company, 1973.

———. *Helicopters and VTOL Aircraft.* New York: Doubleday & Co., 1968.

Thomason, Tommy. "Military Version of XV-15 TiltRotor JVX Program Update." *Rotobreeze* 33 (January 1984).

———. "The History of Helicopters in the U.S. Navy." *Vertiflite,* May/June 1984, pp. 68–74.

Thompson, Robert, ed. *War In Peace.* New York: Harmony Books, 1985.

Tierney, Richard. *The Army Aviation Story.* Northport, Alabama: Colonial Press, 1963.

Torry, John A. H. and Bradford, E. W. "Helicopters Versus Submarines." *Naval Aviation News,* February 1955, pp. 1–5.

Truver, Scott. "Mines of August: an International Whodunit." *U.S. Naval Institute Proceedings,* May 1985.

"Utility-Tactical Transport Helicopter Company (UTTHCO) Unit History." Chronology of Units Deployed to the Republic of Vietnam. Headquarters, U.S. Army Audit Agency, 2 August 1963.

U.S. Army Combat Developments Command. "Annex C: Field Experiments and Troop Test Assessments." Final Report, Army Air Mobility Evaluation, 15 February 1965.

U.S. Army Concept Team In Vietnam. "Armed Helicopters—Monthly Test Report Number Two." Annexes B, C, E, H, K, L, M, N, O and P, 31 December 1962.

Van Vleet, Clarke and Armstrong, William J. *United States Naval Aviation: 1910–1980.* Washington, D.C.: United States Government Printing Office, 1981.

Watson, J. D. "Marine Helicopters—Stunted Growth." *United States Naval Institute Proceedings* 99 (July 1973): 36–41.

Wheeler, Gerald E. "Naval Aviation in the Korean War." *U.S. Naval Institute Proceedings* 83 (July 1957): 762–778.

Williams, D. A. C. "Cierva Air Horse." *Air-Britain Helicopter Research Group Movements Review,* December 1970, pp. 271–273.

Williams, Samuel C. *Report on the Helicopter: The Helicopter and its Role As a Transport Vehicle.* An annotated bibliography sponsored by Brundage Story and Rose Research, Report Series A-1, New York, 1955.

NOTES

Introduction

1 Michael J. Novosel, "From Wood and Linen Kites to Metal Monsters," *United States Army Aviation Digest* 30 (June 1984): 3.
2 Donald F. Harrison, "Developments in Airmobility," *United States Army Aviation Digest* 15 (June 1969): 20.
3 R. J. Arpurt, "Aspects des operations heliportees en Algerie," *Foreces Aeriennes Francaises,* no. 158 (1960), pp. 7–8.
4 Lou Drendel, *Huey* (Carrollton, Texas: Squadron/Signal Publications, 1983), p. 4.
5 Walter J. Boyne and Donald S. Lopez, *Vertical Flight, The Age of the Helicopter* (Washington, D.C.: Smithsonian Institute Press, 1984), pp. 47 and 117.
6 *Flying Magazine,* November 1951, p. 74.
7 Edward J. Bavarvo, "Soviet Helicopter Armament," *Army Aviation Digest,* 30 (November 1984): 37.
8 Arpurt, p. 1.

The Roots of Military Rotary-Wing Aircraft

1 Clarke Van Vleet and William J. Armstrong, *United States Naval Aviation: 1910–1980* (Washington, D.C.: United States Government Printing Office, 1981), p. 6.
2 Ibid.
3 Denis M. Desoutter, *Aircraft and Missiles,* 2nd ed. (New York: John De Graff Inc., 1959), p. 120.
4 Ibid.
5 Robert A. Hasskarl, Jr., "Early Military Use of Rotary-Wing Aircraft," *Airpower Historian,* 12 (July 1965): 75.
6 Frank T. Courtney, *Flight Path: My Fifty Years of Aviation* (London: William Kimber), p. 161.
7 Ibid., p. 163.
8 P. T. Capon, "Cierva's First Autogiros (Part 2)," *Aeroplane Monthly,* 7 (May 1979): 237.
9 B. P. Simmonds, "Thirty Years of Helicopter Flying in the RAF," *Air Clues,* September 1983, p. 347.
10 F. K. Smith, *Legacy of Wings* (New York: Jason Aronson, Inc., 1981).
11 Hasskarl, p. 76.
12 Paul Jackson, "Super Puma," *Air International,* 26 (January 1984): 38.
13 Lyn Montross and Ray Prouty, *U.S. Marine Corps Helicopter Experience,* p. 20.
14 Ibid., p. 21.
15 Harold C. Major, Paul A. Putnam and Frank M. June, "Report to Commanding Officer Aircraft Squadrons, Second Marine Brigade" (Managua, Nicaragua: USMC general file no. 1165-15, 9 November 1932).
16 Montross and Prouty, pp. 25–26.
17 Ibid., pp. 26–27.
18 Hasskarl, p. 76.
19 Ibid.
20 Ibid.
21 Ibid., p. 77.
22 Ibid.
23 Montross and Prouty, p. 27.
24 Ibid., p. 22.

World War II Rotary-Wing Aircraft

1 "A Helicopter for Military Purposes," *Scientific American,* February 26, 1921.
2 Charles Gablehouse, *Helicopters and Autogiros: A History of Rotary-Wing and V/STOL Aviation* (Philadelphia: J. B. Lippincott Company, 1969), p. 60.
3 Harrison, pp. 21–22.
4 Hasskarl, p. 72.
5 Norman Polmar and Floyd D. Kennedy, *Military Helicopters of the World: Military Rotary-Wing Aircraft Since 1917* (Baltimore: Naval Institute Press, 1981), p. 335.
6 Ibid., p. 56.
7 "Henrich Focke's Singular Kite, Part II," *Air International* 26 (June 1984): 291.
8 Ibid., pp. 291–292.
9 Ibid., pp. 292–293.
10 Ibid., p. 292.
11 Ibid., p. 293.
12 Ibid., p. 293–294.
13 H. E. Weimhmiller and H. P. Meiners, "Focke-Achgelis Rotary-Wing Kite," (Report by the Field Information Agency, fiat final report no. 176, 1 October 1945), p. 2.
14 Polmar and Kennedy, p. 61.
15 "Focke's Singular Kite, Part II," p. 294.
16 Ibid.
17 Ibid., p. 296.
18 Drendel, p. 4.
19 Boyne and Lopez, p. 51.
20 Ibid., p. 52.

21 Van Vleet and Armstrong, p. 117.
22 E. B. Potter and Chester W. Nimtz, *Sea Power: A Naval History* (Englewood Cliffs, N.J.: Prentice Hall, 1960), p. 856.
23 Winston S. Churchill, *The Second World War* (Boston: Houghton Mifflin Company, 1948), p. 598.
24 Tommy Thomason, "The History of Helicopters in the U.S. Navy," *Vertiflight*, May/June 1984, p. 68.
25 Potter and Nimitz, p. 553.
26 Van Vleet and Armstrong, p. 122.
27 Ibid., p. 123.
28 Ibid.
29 Thomason, p. 68–69.
30 Ibid., p. 69.
31 Van Vleet and Armstrong, p. 128.
32 Ibid., p. 129.
33 Thomason, p. 70.
34 Ibid., p. 69.
35 Van Vleet and Armstrong, p. 129.
36 Richard Tierney, *The Army Aviation Story* (Northpoint, Alabama: Colonial Press, 1963), p. 204.
37 Ibid., p. 4.
38 Ibid., p. 204.
39 Harrison, p. 22.
40 Tierney, p. 205.
41 Alfred R. Maxwell, "Use of Helicopters for Rescue by the Army Air Forces," Memorandum, February 26, 1946, p. 2.
42 Ibid., p. 1.
43 Ibid.
44 Ibid.
45 Ibid., pp. 1–2.
46 Ibid., p. 2.
47 Ibid.
48 William K. Kay, "The Army Aviation Story," *United States Army Aviation Digest* 7 (June 1961): 4.
49 Ibid.
50 Harrison, p. 22.
51 Van Vleet and Armstrong, p. 129.
52 Ibid., p. 142.
53 Thomason, p. 70.
54 Ibid., p. 69.
55 Ibid., p. 70.
56 Ibid., p. 72.
57 Ibid.
58 Ibid., pp. 70–71.
59 Van Vleet and Armstrong, p. 170.
60 Ibid., p. 173.
61 Jim Mesko, *Airmobile: The Helicopter War in Vietnam* (Carrollton, Texas: Squadron Signal Publications, Inc., 1984), p. 4.
62 B. Franklin Cooling, "A History of U.S. Army Aviation," *Aerospace Historian* 21 (Summer/June 1974): 103.
63 Kay, p. 5.

The Malayan Emergency

1 M. W. Sutcliffe, "Malayan Operations," *U.S. Army Aviation Digest* 8 (October 1962): 10.
2 "Air Operations in the Malay Campaigns," *Aeroplane* 80 (April 20, 1951): 1.
3 Ibid.
4 Bruce E. Harvey, "Casualty Evacuation by Helicopter in Malaya," *British Medical Journal*, no. 4730 (1951), p. 542.
5 "Air Operations in the Malay," p. 1.
6 Harvey, p. 543.
7 Group Captain Slater, "Air Operations in Malaya," *Journal of the Royal United Services Institute for Defense Studies*, August 1957, p. 282.
8 "Air Operations in the Malay," p. 1.
9 Slater, p. 379.
10 Ibid.
11 M. C. Neel and Lt. Col. Spurgeon, "Medical Considerations in Helicopter Evacuation," *U.S. Armed Forces Medical Journal* 5 (February 1954): 2.
12 Harvey, p. 542.
13 Ibid.
14 Jackson, p. 91.
15 Slater, p. 383.
16 John Chartres, *Helicopter Rescue* (Shepperton, England: Ian Allan Ltd., 1980), p. 55.
17 Ibid., p. 57.

18 J. E. Breeze, "Rotors Over the Jungle: Number 848 Naval Air Squadron in Malaya," (Publication Unknown), 12 March 1954, p. 291.
19 Ibid.
20 Ibid.
21 Ibid.
22 Chartres, p. 57.
23 Slater, p. 379.
24 Ibid., p. 380.
25 Ibid.
26 Breeze, p. 1.
27 Breeze, p. 292.
28 Chartres, p. 57.
29 Harvey, p. 543.
30 Breeze, p. 291.
31 Chartres, p. 55.
32 Breeze, p. 292.
33 Slater, p. 384.
34 Ibid.
35 Ibid.
36 Slater, p. 385.

The Korean War

1 J. D. Watson, "Marine Helicopters—Stunted Growth," *United States Naval Institute Proceedings,* 99 (July 1973): 41.
2 Montross and Prouty, p. 109.
3 Ibid., p. 121.
4 Gablehouse, p. 165.
5 David W. Wragg, *Helicopters at War* (London: Robert Hale, 1983), p. 67.
6 Ibid., p. 66.
7 Gerald E. Wheeler, "Naval Aviation In The Korean War," *U.S. Naval Institute Proceedings* 83 (July 1957): 763.
8 Ibid., p. 762.
9 Ibid., p. 765.
10 "Naval Airpower in Korea," *Naval Aviator News,* February 1951, p. 4.
11 Tierney, p. 208.
12 Jackson, p. 84.
13 Ibid., p. 83.
14 Ibid., p. 86.
15 Ibid., p. 87.
16 Ibid.
17 Harrison, p. 22.
18 Cooling, p. 104.
19 Novosel, p. 7.
20 Jackson, p. 89.
21 Ibid., p. 90.
22 Tierney, pp. 208–209.
23 Ibid., pp. 209–210.
24 Kay, p. 5.
25 Gablehouse, p. 164.
26 Harrison, p. 23.
27 Tierney, p. 211.
28 Ibid., p. 214.
29 Ibid.
30 Smith, p. 6.
31 Tierney, p. 212.
32 Ibid.
33 Ibid., p. 214.
34 Harrison, p. 23.
35 Tierney, p. 215.
36 Harrison, p. 23.
37 Bavaro, p. 34.
38 Ibid.
39 Ibid., p. 36.
40 John A. H. Torry and E. W. Bradford, "Helicopters Versus Submarines," *Naval Aviation News,* February 1955, p. 2.
41 Ibid., p. 5.
42 Ibid., pp. 2–3.
43 Ibid., p. 3.
44 Ibid., pp. 2–4.

The French-Algerian War

1 Mesko, p. 4.
2 Arpurt, p.1.
3 David Riley, "French Helicopter Operations in Algeria," *Marine Corps Gazette,* February 1958, p. 22.
4 French Army Aviation Headquarters, "French Airmobility," *U.S. Army Aviation Digest* 21 (March 1975): 4.
5 Ibid., p. 13.
6 Arpurt, p. 22.
7 Bavaro, p. 34.
8 Riley, p. 23.
9 "French Army Helicopter Operations in Algeria, June 1956–September 1959," (Report no. SM-406, 1 November 1959), p. 5.
10 Ibid., p. 79.
11 Ibid., p. 68.
12 Ibid., p. 73–75.
13 Ibid., p. 75.
14 Bavaro, p. 35.
15 Ibid.
16 Riley, p. 24.
17 Ibid.
18 "French Army Helicopter Operations in Algeria," p. 79.
19 Riley, p. 25.
20 "French Army Helicopter Operations in Algeria," p. 81.
21 Ibid.
22 Ibid. pp. 1–4.

Vietnam: The Helicopter War

1 Novosel, p. 9.
2 Cooling, p. 106.
3 Gablehouse, p. 157.
4 Mesko, p. 9.
5 John J. Tolson, *Airmobility, 1961–1971* (Washington, D.C.: Department of the Army, 1973).
6 Gablehouse, p. 158.
7 Carl Berger, ed., *The United States Air Force in Southeast Asia, 1961–1973: An Illustrated Account* (Washington, D.C.: U.S. Government Printing Office, 1977), p. 19.
8 Watson, p. 40.
9 Mesko, p. 16.
10 Watson, p. 40.
11 U.S. Army Audit Agency, "Utility Tactical Transport Helicopter Company (UTTHCO) Unit History," 2 August 1963, pp. 197–207.
12 U.S. Army, "UTTHCO Staff Office Report," October–December 1962, p. 4.
13 "OPENAH Monthly Report Number Two, 16 November–15 December 1962," 31 December 1962.
14 Regulation Number 55-12, Helicopter Escort, Headquarters, Second Air Division, 27 December 1962, pp. 1–4.
15 U.S. Army Combat Developments Command, "Annex C: Field Experiments and Troop Test Assessments," (Final Report, Army Air Mobility Evaluation, 15 February 1965), p. C2-3-7.
16 U.S. Army Concept Team in Vietnam, "Armed Helicopters—Monthly Test Report Number Two, Annex B," p. 1.
17 Ibid., p. 2.
18 Mesko, p. 9.
19 Harrison, p. 23.
20 Ibid.
21 Cooling, p. 105.
22 Harrison, p. 24.
23 Ibid.
24 Ibid.
25 "General Kinnard's Official Biography," unpublished, U.S. Army Historical Center, Washington, D.C., July 1967.
26 Gablehouse, p. 154.
27 U.S. Army Concept Team in Vietnam, "Monthly Test Report Number Two, Annex N," p. 2.
28 Cooling, p. 107.
29 Gablehouse, p. 161.
30 Peter B. Mersky, *U.S. Marine Corps Aviation, 1912 to the Present* (Baltimore: The Nautical and Aviation Publishing Company of America, 1983), p. 242.
31 Berger, p. 238.
32 Ibid., p. 239.
33 Ibid., p. 243.
34 "Assault Helo Office Open (at Naval Air Systems Command)," *Naval Aviation News,* 1968, p. 2.
35 Peter B. Mersky and Norman Polmar, *The Naval Air War in Vietnam* (Baltimore: The Nautical and Aviation Publishing Company of America, 1981), p. 208.
36 Mesko, p. 62.

Developments in the Soviet Union

1 John Everett-Heath, *Soviet Helicopters* (London: Jane's Publishing Company Limited, 1983).
2 Jackson, p. 73.
3 Norman Polmar, "JVX," *U.S. Naval Institute Proceedings,* November 1983, p. 124.
4 Bill Gunston, *Helicopters at War* (London: The Hamlyn Publishing Group Limited, 1977), p. 120.
5 Bavaro, p. 36.
6 Charles M. Thomas, "Update of Soviet Helicopters," *U.S. Army Aviation Digest* 30 (July 1984): pp. 16–18.
7 *Soviet Military Power,* 1983 ed., (Washington, D.C.: Department of Defense).
8 Bavaro, p. 36.
9 *Air Clues,* July 1983, p. 243.
10 Bronislaw Maca, "Soviet Aviation: A Fly-by-Night Operation," *U.S. Army Aviation Digest,* May 1973, pp. 37–39.
11 James C. Harris, "Theater Level Implications of Armed Helicopter Threats," *Amphibious Warfare Review,* 2 (July 1984): 46, 102–103.
12 Thomas, pp. 17–18.
13 Richard N. Papworth, "Soviet Navy Reactions to the Falkland Island Conflict," *Naval War College Review,* 38 (March–April 1985): 53–72.
14 "HIND and Seek," *Defense Helicopter Review* 5 (August/September 1986): 33.
15 Drew Middleton, "Afganistan: Soviets Learn From Rebels," *New York Times,* 23 January 1983, p. 1.
16 *Soviet Military Power,* 1986 ed., (Washington, D.C.: Department of Defense).
17 *Defence Helicopter World,* August/September 1986, p. 33.

Fighting Helicopters of the 1980s

1 "The Re-occupation of South Georgia," *Flight Deck,* Falklands Edition, 1982, p. 31.
2 Ibid., p. 32.
3 Ibid., p. 7.
4 Vic Flintham, "Invasion of Grenada," *Air Pictorial* 47 (January 1985): 8.
5 Frank Brewer, "HMM-261 Grenada Operations," (Oral presentation at the Naval Helicopter Association 37th Annual Symposium, Virginia Beach, Va., 2 May 1985).
6 Flintham, p. 11.
7 "Grenada Gamble," *Aviation Week and Space Technology,* 31 October 1983, p. 17.
8 Brewer, oral presentation.
9 Flintham, p. 11.
10 Ibid.

Combat Missions: The 1990s and Beyond

1 Tommy Thomason, "The History of Helicopters in the U.S. Navy," *Vertiflite,* May/June 1984, p. 74.
2 *Aviation Week and Space Technology,* 23 October 1972.
3 Barvaro, p. 37.
4 E. H. Grayson, Jr., "Army Aviation 1984 to 2015," *Army Aviation Digest* 28 (July 1982): 3.
5 *AMCM Tow Tales,* Airborne Mine Countermeasures Program Division Newsletter, Naval Air Systems Command (Washington, D.C.): December 1984, p. 6.
6 Ibid., pp. 5–7.
7 Bavaro, p. 3.
8 Paul G. Fahlstrom, "Air-to-Air Missiles for Marine Corps and Army Helicopters," *Amphibious Warfare Review* 2 (July 1984): 19.
9 Defence Helicopter Review, June/August 1984, p. 101.
10 Bavaro, p. 37.
11 D. Laskin, "Pax River Teams Studying Copters in Aerial Combat," *Navy Times,* 11 July 1983, p. 17.
12 Fahlstrom, p. 19.
13 Ibid., p. 18.
14 Ibid., p. 19.
15 "Bell Advanced Tilt Rotor (BAT): Possible Entry to Army LHX Program," *Rotorbreeze* 33 (July/August 1984): 3.
16 American Helicopter Society, "Vertical Flight's Relevance in Defense," report to members, Fall 1985.

INDEX